MIRRORS OF THE MIND:

Personal Construct Theory in the Training of Adult Educators

PHILIP C. CANDY

**Department of Adult and Higher Education,
University of Manchester.**

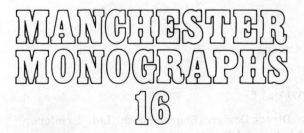

MANCHESTER
MONOGRAPHS
16

©   P.C. Candy

April 1981

ISBN 0 903717 25 5

Printed by: Direct Design (Bournemouth) Ltd. Printers,
Butts Pond Industrial Estate, Sturminster Newton, Dorset, DT10 1AZ

CONTENTS

iii

CONTENTS

v

PREFACE

It must be a common experience for writers to review their finished work and to reflect on all the things which they have failed to treat adequately. Indeed, it is rare to pick up a text book or other piece of academic work, in which the author does not lament the rapid effluxion of time, or list some of the unopened doors, and the unanswered questions which their labours have revealed. I am, therefore, in good company when I begin by saying that I feel dissatisfied; not so much with what I have said, but with all that which, through misapprehension, misjudgement, or the limitations of time and space, I have left unsaid.

Although my primary focus is on the development of adult educators,

> ...I have tried, throughout, to bear in mind the broader picture, to take some account of the literature which refers to it, to indicate the common ground. Others must judge whether there is enough of this to be of some use to other educators... in addition to my own immediate colleagues. I should like to think so, and venture to claim that, at least, there are enough links left open into which others may be encouraged to mesh their considerations of the broader field.
>
> (Elsdon, 1975, p 7)

The idea for this monograph grew out of a remarkable and stimulating year spent as a student at Manchester in 1978/9. I have been assisted in writing it by countless people, and in a variety of ways. Firstly, there is the legion of authors, many of them mentioned in the References, whose works have contributed so much to my understanding. Secondly, like all adult educators, I own an immense debt to my colleagues, particularly in Australia and Britain, whose stimulating comments and discussion not infrequently resulted in valuable insights which might otherwise have eluded me, Finally, there are those people whose contribution to this project has been more specific, and whilst it is difficult, and perhaps invidious, to single out some for particular mention, I would especially like to express my gratitude and appreciation to the following people.

Mike Toye, who first introduced me to Kelly's Personal Construct Theory during a course of lectures on Learning Theory and, despite a heavy workload, also found time to read my initial manuscript and offer many helpful suggestions for improvement.

Brian Nichol, my tutor, encouraged me to explore the previously unknown territory of Personal Constructs, and made many valuable suggestions, particularly directing me to several relevant books and studies, which would otherwise have escaped my notice. In relation to this monograph, he also encouraged me to persist at times when my commitment to the task was flagging, and has cheerfully handled the administrative and editorial difficulties of liaising halfway round the world.

Mrs Pat Hurst, the Departmental Librarian, was unfailingly cheerful, and more than once somehow caused needed books to materialise, seemingly out of thin air. I would like also to acknowledge the patience and skill of two typists, Mrs Hilda Gaddum and Mrs Marion Bele, both of whom managed to decipher my scrawl, and to produce expertly typed copy from a patchwork of handwritten and typed originals.

Last, but certainly not least, my wife Mary-Anne, who helped me in more ways than she will ever know; from inventing diversions for the entertainment of our two small children, to listening patiently as I struggled to give form to those vague and shadowy ideas which pass for understanding.

Despite the debts owed to all these people, the final responsibility for this monograph is entirely my own.

PHILIP C. CANDY

Adelaide
July 1980

INTRODUCTION

> It could be claimed that the fundamental development of the last fifteen years in this field (adult education) was the gradual realisation that history, tradition, practical know-how, ideology and sectional claims and counter-claims were not tantamount to professional knowledge. It was further realised that this knowledge needed to be more than a collection of relevant extracts from the canons of psychology, sociology and philosophy which would serve adult education's turn by inserting the prefix 'educational' or the suffix 'of adult education'. It came to be felt that adult educators needed to draw on the insights, skills and methods of these and other disciplines in order to study their own experience of teaching, organising and training. Upon that ground, they would build a new and independent synthesis.
>
> (Elsdon, 1975, p 7)

It is quite possible to teach without formal teacher training; for instance. parents have successfully been teaching their children, and masters their apprentices, since time bagan. However, from the time of the first Monastic training schools, and the consequent emergence of full-time, professional pedagogues, there has been a growing conviction that the quality of teaching can be enhanced by the systematic study and mastery of certain basic concepts and skills. It is upon this single fundamental assumption that the whole massive super-structure of teacher training and trainer training throughout the world has been erected.

Whilst there is widespread agreement amongst teacher educators at this sort of philosophical level, they diverge sharply from one another on practical questions concerning how to go about the business of developing teachers. For a start, there is very little agreement as to what constitutes effective teaching (or indeed even about how it might be recognised) and as a result, little agreement concerning how student teachers ought to be trained in order to be effective. Naturally, therefore, programmes of teacher training and in-service development vary immensely - reflecting an enormous diversity of aims, methods and content. The preferred mode of enquiry to be pursued by student teachers is debated endlessly, as are the precepts and abilities which they are encouraged to master.

The development of adult educators is more complex still, for it draws not only on the established philosophy and traditions of teacher training generally, but also on the expanding body of theory about how adults learn best, and consequently, how their learning might best be facilitated. The point is, that if adult educators are being acquainted with a body of knowledge about how adults learn and should be taught, the process must be congruent with the content.

This monograph, then, enters a field already filled to overflowing with competing ideas, plans, programmes, methods, approaches and objectives. However, it is my contention that two main criticisms can be levelled at teacher education generally, and a third one at the training of teachers in adult, further and higher education in particular. Naturally enough, since the points are more or less independent of each other, I do not intend to imply that they always occur together, nor that they are necessarily true, either individually or collectively, of every programme of teacher training or development.

The first criticism is that teacher training often fails to account adequately for the personal predispositions, and significant informal preparation for teaching, of people newly entering the service. This is particularly true of teachers entering the field of adult or further education, often with years of experience in commerce, industry or government.

My second criticism is that too often teacher training is carried on at the intellectual, cognitive, and 'public' level, with insufficient attention being paid to the critical importance of allowing the student teacher to inspect his or her own beliefs and assumptions about teaching and learning. Furthermore, it is my observation that mechanisms need to be developed which facilitate the linking of new learning into these established patterns of thought and action.

Thirdly, I believe that the substantial empirical findings about how adults learn best, tend to be more honoured in the breach than in the observance, when it comes to actually conducting learning programmes for adult educators.

Linking these three ideas together, it is my contention that all people who work as teachers, whether newly entered or with years of experience, have carefully elaborated schemes for perceiving the activity of teaching (which in turn form part of their total view of reality) and furthermore that they have well established, and highly individual, strategies for acquiring new learning. What is required, I believe, is a methodology which encourages reflection and self-awareness, which is congruent with adult learning principles, and which takes into account the individual learner's pre-existing pattern of values, attitudes, and understandings.

It is the thesis of this monograph that Kelly's Repertory Grid Technique represents one such methodology, and that the quality of courses for the professional development of adult educators may be improved by the use of this Technique.

CHAPTER I

THE TRAINING OF ADULT EDUCATORS

It would seem that in the last ten or fifteen years, the vast, amorphous and deeply interconnected field which we call adult education has experienced a meteoric rise to prominence, in most parts of the world. Details vary from country to country, but participation rates generally have lifted significantly, government funding has likewise increased, courses and organisations for the professional training and development of adult educators have proliferated, research and publications in the field have expanded dramatically.

There are many reasons for this trend. In part, it is a reflection of the impact of rapid social and technological change, causing adults to seek out retraining or further training in trades and professions, in part it reflects changed patterns of leisure and recreation, whilst other factors include increased demand for basic literacy and numeracy skills, the requirement to be able to participate more fully in civic and community affairs; in short to become more fully human.

Committees of Enquiry and Offices of Statistics generate more, and more comprehensive, reports - the situation is similar in Britain, Canada, Australia, The United States and elsewhere. And all this frantic activity has occurred in a marginal, fragmented and dissolute field, legendary for its traditions of voluntarism, amateurism and evangelism.

One important corollary of this phenomenal growth and increased awareness of adult education, has been the demand for more, and better trained, adult educators. The term 'adult educator' is open to many alternative interpretations, and it is fairly widely accepted that adult education occurs in a tremendous range of settings. The following scheme distinguishes adult educators according to the breadth of their responsibility, rather than the field in which they happen to work.

> At the apex of the pyramid is the (small) group of those who have made adult education the focus of their careers, and who intend to spend their lifetime as specialists in it. They include

those responsible for directing the adult education activities of
universities, churches, community colleges, public schools,
libraries, museums, industries, argicultural organisations,
government departments and a host of social agencies ...

At the intermediate level are those whose adult educational
service is part of their regular job, or who accept supplemental
employment in that field. Among them are evening class teachers, public librarians, museum curators, art gallery officers
and specialists in business or the professions...

The broad base of the pyramid, and by far its largest component,
comprises adult education's lay leaders. Virtually all adult
education agencies make use of laymen as volunteers, paid or
unpaid...

(Campbell, 1977, p 38)

This last category, the vast army of 'part-time tutors' (Elsdon, 1975)
is generally described in the following terms:

...most untrained for the work; transient; poorly paid; mostly
inexperienced; mostly voluntary or part-time workers; not
receiving any inservice training; out of contact with similar
workers in other agencies; do not regard adult education as a
career; will probably quit this year...

(Grabowski, 1976, p 2)

Clearly, the training and developmental needs of people occupying these
various levels of responsibility will differ, though most authorities (for
instance, Campbell, 1977; Elsdon, 1975) see the need for some sort of
developmental sequence and logical career path in order to encourage
adult educators to progress through a cumulative programme of studies.

The development of courses and programmes for adult educators has
been retarded, in many respects, by the widespread assumption that
adult education is not a field of study in its own right. It is hard to know
precisely when a discipline or field of study has 'arrived', but it seems
safe to assume that so long as its own practitioners continue to refer to
their area as 'incipient' or 'embryonic', then it still is. In 1964,
Jensen, Liveright and Hallenbeck edited a book entitled Adult Education:
Outlines of an Emerging Field of University Study. Thirteen years later,
in 1977, Campbell wrote;

It is today aptly described as an emerging field of study which
draws much of its substance from the social sciences, and
which is in the process of establishing a theory base within itself. Indeed, the considerable extent of that theory base has
encouraged Apps and Boyd (1976) to take the position that adult
education has its own unique structure and function which give it
identity... (though) apart from the formulation of principles and
generalisations from practice, adult education in the main has
been expanded as a field of study through the borrowing and
reformulation of knowledge from other disciplines.

(Campbell, 1977, pp 72-3)

Irrespective of how it got to its present state of development, there are
now University level courses in adult and continuing education throughout Britain, Canada, the United States, New Zealand, Australia and
many other countries besides, though the nature and content of these
courses varies enormously.

Whilst it is outside the scope of this monograph to review the many
innovative programmes and models which have been developed for
training teachers of adults, it is worth drawing attention to an important
distinction which allows different approaches to be roughly grouped on
one very basic criterion, viz: the degree to which learning outcomes are
specified.

According to Elsdon, writing in a British context:

There are, in fact, no typical or ideal characteristics for adult
educators, and it would be unwise to try and devise them. Even
'enthusiasm' and a 'sense of humour', which seem to figure with
such monotonous regularity in various proclamations and advert-
isements are, like an absence of nervousness in teachers,
neither necessary nor teachable...

(Elsdon, 1975, p 103)

According to Campbell, however:

...this, emphatically, is not the view of his American counter-
parts, who have set out the competencies, essential behaviours,
qualities, knowledge and skills and essential leadership characteristics of adult educators in almost redundant detail...

(Campbell, 1977, p 53)

This dichotomy is neither new, nor restricted to the training of adult educators, but in fact is a perennial argument which plagues the training of teachers in general. Each of these viewpoints has its adherents, and each has given rise to, or acts as the philosophical underpinning for, a number of courses of teacher education. On the one hand, there is the liberal studies or 'great ideas' sort of model which rests on the assumption that the main purpose of teacher education is to encourage trainee teachers to be more introspective, philosophical and self-aware and, on the other hand, what is loosely called the competency-based approach, which "places the competencies required for successful performance beyond the academic programme and at the front and centre of the learning and credentialling processes. This makes the demonstration of competence under realistic conditions the indispensable requirement for awarding credentials" (Grabowski, 1976, p 7).

> Each of these approaches has its drawbacks. In this day and age, the problem with the 'great ideas' model (i. e. the notion that exposure to great ideas in the field would be sufficient to develop a trainee teacher into a truly educated person and fully functioning teacher) is that it tends to overemphasize the individual development of the person, and fails to account for the increasing complexity of technical knowledge and professional performances related to specific occupations. Conversely, the problem in the competency model is that it may neglect the essential development of the individual with respect to his/her profession, and instead operationalize the professional performances with such a degree of specificity, that it fails to develop the holistic competencies of the professional.
>
> (Hobart, 1979, p 16)

Hobart goes on to propose an integration of the two approaches:

> In such a system, the body of knowledge available is focused upon the planning, implementing and evaluating responsibilities of the professional teacher... At the same time, the more personal development of the individual student teacher with respect to professional competence is acheived through constant focus on self-monitoring, self-correction and self-renewal.
>
> (Hobart, 1979, pp 16-17)

The intriguing point is that some sort of compromise, or middle road, almost seems demanded by the situation itself. Even the most ardent apologists for the different views, seem implicitly to accept at least in

part the legitimacy of the alternative. Elsdon, for instance though
maintaining that there are no ideal characteristics or skills, writes:

> There was a common assumption that knowledge of a subject
> was equivalent to an ability to teach it, a touching faith that
> teaching, because it is subtle, personal and depends on relation-
> ships, does not involve any skills which can be defined and
> taught.
>
> (Elsdon, 1975, p 12)

He describes this assumption as a 'dubious proposition', and by implication there are indeed some "skills which can be defined and taught",
though they are rather buried in the text of Elsdon's work. Conversely,
in the various lists of suggested (and usually highly specific) competencies, often appear items such as:

> Knowledge of his own values, strengths and weaknesses
>
> (Chamberlain, 1961)

and

> He should possess a mature and progressively developing
> philosophy of education
>
> (Houle, 1957)

It would seem, then, that even in their 'pure' form, both the 'great
ideas' model and the more specific 'competency-based' approach share
the common ultimate objective:

> to enable the adult educator to knit together, in a unity of his
> own devising, those insights, skills and methods from...
> subjects which are unequivocally relevant to adult education.
>
> (Campbell, 1977, p 80)

or, in other words

> to develop a personal, working philosophy of adult education.
>
> (Apps, 1973)

This monograph has the same objective. It is not concerned with the
content of programmes for the professional development of adult educators. Instead, it addresses a strategy whereby trainee teachers might
be encouraged to reflect on their own structures of meaning, to explore
and perhaps modify, their personal and professional value systems.

Whilst it is perfectly true that the Repertory Grid Technique described in this monograph can be used to advantage in any programme for training teachers of adults, it is unambiguously based on a social phenomenological perspective and is likely to be most congruent with approaches which emphasise self direction in adult learning (Knowles, 1975).

CHAPTER II

KEY PROBLEMS IN TEACHER EDUCATION

"No man in his senses will ever deny the inexplicable, seamless mystery that is good teaching and effective learning," writes Elsdon, (p 6) and it could just as well be said that only the brave or the foolish would ever claim to have discovered the secret of successful teacher education. The number and range of approaches to this perennial area of concern bear witness to the creativity, innovativeness and professionalism of those charged with the responsibility of turning people into well trained and effective teachers. Yet, despite many years of experimentation, there are still many unsolved problems and unresolved dilemmas.

In this chapter, I propose to focus on two such problem areas - the influence of 'natural teaching style', and integration of theory and practice. A third contentious area, that of striving for congruence between what is said and what is done in the training and development of adult educators, is dealt with separately in Chapter IV of this monograph.

NATURAL TEACHING STYLE

From time to time, teacher educators are assailed by doubts as to whether they are really making any significant difference to the way in which their student teachers perform. To be sure, they can observe their protégés using aids of various sorts, producing lesson plans, employing a range of tricks and techniques, occasionally even excelling themselves and appearing actually to engage their learners, but there is still that nagging doubt. It is not so much the lingering suspicion that teachers are born, not made, but rather a subtle variant on the same theme - the vague notion that there are some underlying differences which predispose certain people to be better or more effective teachers than others.

Few teacher educators would argue with the notion that teachers in training may have certain attitudes, abilities, characteristics and preconceptions which are likely to influence how they teach. The contentious part is the extent to which these things are themselves directly influenced by teacher education. If there are variables which significantly influence how someone teaches, and if teacher training fails to account for these variables at all, then a strong case can be made that teacher training is less than fully effective.

To describe this phenomenon, the term 'natural' teaching style has been used. As this term may cause some concern, an attempt will be made to explain what it is intended to mean. Bennett does use the phrase, but without making explicit what he means by it:

> ... it would appear that teachers take little cognisance of... literature in determining their natural teaching style. This fact was noted in the Plowden Report which considered that it was rare to find teachers who had given much time to the study of educational theory, even in their College of Education days.
>
> (Bennett, 1976, p 37)

By implication, the process of teacher training is expected to result in some modification of 'natural' teaching style, or at least in the integration of certain theoretical considerations in the teacher's characteristic mode of teaching.

The phrase 'teaching style' has been used by different writers to signify different things; to some it means teaching methods, to others a teacher's philospphy, and to others again it might be analogous to 'personal style'. Edward de Bono has this to say about style:

> Style is important but intangible. We can recognise it and say a lot about it, except what it really is. For instance, some painters have a style that is easily recognisable. Consistency is probably the key element in style. We may not be able to predict exactly what will happen any more than we could predict what a painter will paint, but we may be able to predict the style in which it will be done. Consistency means that the way something is done fits the style of the person or situation, but it also means that each part of what is done fits in exactly with all the other parts. It is this fitting together that establishes the style.
>
> (de Bono, 1979, p 232)

In this context, teaching style may be defined as:
    those recurrent and habitual patterns of teaching behaviours

(strategies, methods, approaches and responses) which manifest and are based upon the individual teacher's personal and professional philosophy.

Finally, in using the word 'natural' in this way, it is not intended to exclude other factors such as the emulation of others (either consciously or otherwise) or the influence of prevailing organisational climate, nor indeed to imply that trained teachers are in some way 'unnatural'! 'Natural' teaching style means simply the practices of someone in a teaching role, who has not had the benefit of formal teacher training. In other words, if a person is put into the role of a teacher, he/she will behave in certain ways, and the sum total of those behaviours may loosely be called a teaching style. If the person has not had exposure to formal teacher training, then what he/she does, will reflect a 'natural' teaching style.

What, then, are the main characteristics of a teaching style? Or, more importantly, what are the 'cultural' variables which influence how someone teaches? This is not an easy question to answer, because of the sheer complexity of the teacher's role. It involves, inter alia, social and technical skills, subject knowledge and professional expertise, instantaneous decision making and long term planning, leadership, responsiveness, interpersonal competence and organisation. Researchers have consistently demonstrated the mind-bending complexity of even a single period in the classroom, the difficulty of adequately analysing and specifying the total set of behaviours in teaching is astronomical. However, over a period of time, a number of factors which influence how particular individuals teach, have been isolated.

Some of them are external to the person, and act on trained and untrained teachers alike. These include: the predominant teaching strategies used in the particular institution, the management style and indeed total 'climate' prevailing in the organisation, the expectations of learners as to their preferred mode of 'being taught' (though this more often than not reflects the extent to which learners have adapted themselves to 'being taught', rather than 'learning'), and, as Bernstein maintains, the very way the subject matter is framed and coded by social convention.

Conversely, there are other, internal influences which emanate unmistakeably from within the individual, or impinge most directly on him or her: past experience, personal learning style, personality, intuition, metaphorical models of learning, basic existential position, self-concept, and ideological assumptions about the purposes of education, and processes of teaching. Researchers have at one time or another, linked each of these with teaching, but the fact that none of them yields a perfect correlation with teaching style may be a reflection of imperfect measurement either of the factor or of teaching style, or quite possibly both. More likely, however, is the notion that teaching style is not caused by any single variable, but rather by the dynamic interaction of many.

Unfortunately, there is not the opportunity in this monograph to review all the literature in which these various influences have been connected, either implicitly or explicitly with how people teach, although the author has done so elsewhere.* Given, however, that there are links (whose strength and relative importance vary from person to person), it is not difficult to imagine how conventional programmes of teacher education cope with the various factors. Some, such as 'past experience', are simply too complex for the teacher education programme to take into account – and anyway, how can the salient features of past experience possibly be isolated? Ideological assumptions and, to a lesser extent, metaphorical models of learning, are considered fair game. However, as will be discussed later in this chapter, there are manifold problems in trying to find out what people really think and even once they are out in the public arena, they tend to be highly resistant to change. Items like personality and basic existential position are simply too dangerous. Anna Freud has written:

> I hold we are right in demanding that the teacher or educator should have learned to know and to control his own conflicts before he begins his educational work. If this is not so, the pupils merely serve as more or less suitable material on which to abreact his own unconscious and unsolved difficulties.
>
> (Freud, 1960, p 106)

Although the substance of teaching is human interaction, very few teacher education programmes concentrate on providing student teachers

---

*   See 'Natural Teaching Style: The Forgotten Foundation' in Candy, P.C: The use of Repertory Grid Technique in the Development of Adult Educators, unpublished M.Ed. Dissertation, University of Manchester, 1979.

with systematic and objective data about themselves and their effects on others. On the other hand, to their credit, teacher educators have tended to stay away from any attempt to prescribe 'appropriate' psychological outlooks or desirable personality characteristics as preconditions for teaching success.

Trowbridge's work on self concept marks an interesting contrast. She found a fairly high correlation between teacher self concept and healthy, growthful teaching strategies. In her conclusion, Trowbridge says:

> The evidence seems to indicate that a measure of a teacher's self-concept may tell us much about the way she teaches. Attempts to strengthen teacher self-concept may well encourage divergent and evaluative thinking in the classroom along with the tendency to decrease the amount of time spent in routine. Moreover, it may give students a chance to talk more.
>
> (Trowbridge, 1973, p 140)

In the light of such findings, it is somewhat disappointing to recognise the small number of teacher education programmes which explicitly and overtly set out to enhance the self-concept of student teachers - indeed the reverse is not infrequently the case (albeit unintentionally).

Intuition as a way of selecting teaching strategies was reported by Joyce and Harutoonian in their 1964 study of student teachers. As it stands, it is rather too imprecise as a basis for discussion in teacher education and indeed in all probability, it is a convenient explanation for one or other of the possibilities mentioned here (e.g. the subconscious influence of learning style or of personality.) Recent research into the specialisation of functions within the brain is of interest here. One side of the brain has been found to be largely responsible for logical, analytical, linear, verbal activities, whilst the other side specialises in visual, creative, intuitive, relational and imaginative tasks. (Ornstein, 1975). It is conceivable that the intuitive and holistic functions of the right hemisphere are critical to the act of teaching, but that they are simply not susceptible to analysis, even by an individual looking at his/her own process, much less by an outside researcher looking in.

Lastly, personal learning (or cognitive) style has been linked to teaching style by both Pask and Witkin, but their findings seem not to be widely known amongst teacher educators who, in any case, tend to regard learning styles as a fairly minor influence in determining how people teach, and therefore do not place much emphasis on it.

Out of all these findings and connections comes the conviction that teaching is not a conscious controlled and objective 'performance', but rather that it is a subjective activity, and thus an expression of 'self'; that it is a behavioural manifestation of that complicated and deeply interconnected pattern of beliefs, values, assumptions, experiences, attitudes and insights which might otherwise be called the 'person'. If this is accepted, it becomes relatively meaningless to attempt to separate out the act of teaching from the teacher. Ironically, this is precisely the sort of divorce which conventional teacher education has attempted to force onto teaching. What is more, it is now possible to view all the variables cited here as different aspects of the same entity – the person.

Another particularly important result flows from accepting this point of view. If teaching is recognised as one expression of the person of the teacher, then anything which impinges on the person, might potentially influence his/her teaching, and this demands another look at something which was dismissed earlier. At the beginning of this section, I specifically excluded factors which I described as external to the individual – things like the teaching approaches used by colleagues, or those demanded by students. But who is to say that they are external? Where one teacher might ignore or dismiss the preferences of students, for another these might constitute the ultimate determinant of acceptability and hence success. One teacher might find him/her self influenced to adopt teaching methods which enjoy particular vogue amongst his/her fellow teachers, whereas another is quite able to defend his/her 'deviant' methods, and will continue to employ teaching strategies which do not find favour amongst his/her colleagues. Clearly, what is important is not the factor itself, but its perceived relevance and importance to the individual teacher.

In introducing the idea of 'natural' teaching style, it is not argued that people can teach just as well (or better) without formal training as with it. What I do want to establish is that everyone who enters the teaching profession already holds many deep-seated views and opinions, and is subject to many influences, which inevitably act as a backdrop to their preparation and activity as teachers. Furthermore, there is considerable evidence to suggest that conventional teacher training does not significantly influence these factors. It is my contention, that if teacher training is to be truly effective, then it must concern itself with surfacing and exploring some of these tacit dimensions, and placing greater emphasis on the phenomenological universe, or personally constructed reality, of the individual teacher.

THEORY AND PRACTICE IN EDUCATION

The practice of teaching is as old as mankind. The passing-on of culture, folklore, language, useful skills, and the million and one things which distinguish man from 'lower animals', is an educational activity which has gone on for centuries. Today, we enjoy an immensely complex educational system, commanding vast resources and involving a significant proportion of people's lives, especially in their early years, but increasingly in adulthood as well.

However, the practice of teaching purely as the preserve of the trained professional is a comparatively recent phenomenon. Until recent times, most teaching was carried out by employers, churchmen, parents and other community members, and the qualified professional was a rarity. According to Wragg, this:

> education and training based on nothing but each individual's perception of how (people) learn, produced stereotyped and ineffective teaching.
>
> (Wragg, 1974, p 21)

In an effort to avoid such 'stereotyped and ineffective teaching' and in particular in order to save teachers from making the same mistakes as their predecessors, programmes of teacher education have been evolved.

Early approaches to the question of teacher education rested largely on the apprenticeship model - the notion firstly that teaching was an art, and secondly that the best way to learn an art was by observing and emulating the master. This approach, however has its problems. Gallagher notes that "it is hard to imitate the true artist, and his genius too often dies with him..." (Gallagher, 1970, p 30) Stolurow goes further:

> ...This idea of modelling the master teacher has not worked... One potentially important factor working against this approach is the complexity of the behaviour observed and the associated difficulties of controlling behaviour so that it can be studied. Observations of teaching produce an effect which can be associated with the Rorschach and other projective tests in that different factors are identified by different observers, and each observer interprets what he sees in a different way.
>
> (Stolurow, 1972, p 166)

Besides these difficulties, there was a growing conviction that teaching was not quite as mysterious and intuitive as some had thought – "Those interested in the improvement of education and teaching would like to remove some of the mystery of the art of effective teaching through systematic study." (Gallagher, 1970, p 30)

Half a century ago, Whitehead laid the foundations for a science of teaching when he wrote that a craft "is an avocation based on customary actions and modified by trial and error of individual practice", whereas a profession is "an avocation whose activities are subject to theoretical analysis, and are modified by theoretical conclusions derived from that analysis." (Whitehead, 1929, p 65)

Teachers, anxious to establish their status as professionals, thus grasped at the idea of theoretical consistency to underpin their work, and so began the long search for some single all-embracing theory, and even for the 'one right way' to teach. (This is sometimes referred to as the 'Myth of the Single Method')

Underlying this search for a theory (either of teaching or learning) was the assumption that some aspects of the teaching/learning situation could be isolated, distilled and transmitted to student teachers for them to 'apply' in teaching situations. Bigge expresses the rationale in these terms;

> a teacher need not base his thinking on tradition and folklore.
> Instead, he(she) may be quite aware of the most important
> theories developed by professional educational psychologists,
> in which case his own psychological theory is likely to be quite
> sophisticated. The latter state of affairs is what professional
> psychologists interested in education of teachers are trying to
> induce. Teachers who are well grounded in scientific psychology,
> in contrast to 'folklore psychology', have a basis for making
> decisions that are much more likely to lead to effectual results
> in classrooms.
>
> (Bigge, 1971, p 5)

However, there has been a steady accumulation of evidence to suggest that merely begin "well grounded in scientific psychology" is not enough to ensure "effectual results in classrooms". In this section of the monograph, therefore, I will briefly review some of the attempts which have been made to discover a theory to underpin educational practice, and I will examine a second, but related, problem, viz; whether, and how, trainee teachers integrate such theoretical understandings into their individual practice as teachers.

The Search for a Theory

At a very general level, the search for a theory may be subdivided into those approaches which concentrate on learning, and those which concentrate on teaching. In the first case, an enormous number of investigations has been undertaken (often using non-human subjects in laboratory settings, or else human subjects in non-classroom environments) in the search for principles which could be applied by practising teachers. The second situation involves investigating the practices and beliefs of successful and effective teachers, again looking for patterns and principles upon which their success might be based.

In the pages which follow, a very brief review of these two approaches is attempted, and it is argued that, whilst such studies have generated a great many useful insights into teaching and learning, it is doubtful whether this knowledge significantly influences the practices of trainee teachers.

The Study of Learning

Once teaching and learning became a subject of scientific enquiry, researchers (in the classic natural science paradigm) were concerned with identifying a nexus between cause and effect. Since the effect of teaching is presumably to increase learning (whether this means growth, or enlightenment) in someone else, most researchers were interested in producing a theory of learning. This seems rational:

> It appears logical to study the learning process of the (student), before we determine how we shall teach him.
> (Pittenger and Gooding, 1971, p 70)

This statement is in fact deceptively simple, however, for whilst all teaching methods are based on our understanding of the learning process, educational practice stands supported, as it were, by the twin pillars of learning theory and the teacher's understanding of the purposes of education. In fact, Pittenger and Gooding in their book reproduce a conceptual hierarchical model of educational practice, in which educational philosophy is shown as the basis upon which interpretation of the learning process is build, and this actually puts the study of learning into its proper perspective. As Toye points out, the historical development of theories of learning is virtually inseparable

from the mainstream of psychological enquiry as a whole, and has therefore suffered the same demoralising inconclusiveness:

> "Human behaviour is jolly difficult; we really must do something
> about it. Some of the chaps are so fed up that they have gone
> over to physiology. Still, this new electronic conditioning gadget
> is awfully good fun."

> After fifty years of scientific psychology, some people might
> feel disappointed.

> (Toye, 1973, p 6)

In large measure, this is an inevitable reflection of the diverse
approaches in research methodologies; basic philosophical stances in
relation to man's inherent activity/passivity, and fundamental moral
nature; and the level and type of behaviour observed. Once again, Toye
succinctly caricatures the failure of studies of learning in the natural
science paradigm:

> Other empirical studies, the Sciences, may inhabit grandly
> designed mansions of theory which house rich collections of
> authenticated facts but Psychology has never seemed able to
> manage more than a makeshift sprawl of temporary huts,
> constantly being wrecked by their noisy inhabitants as they
> dispute each others' findings.

> (Toye, 1973, p 1)

In reviewing the literature on learning, it is easy to despair of ever
finding a basic framework on which researchers might agree. Whilst
some theories are 'poles apart', others are really fairly similar to
one another, distinguished only by emphasis or extent, rather than
fundamental differences in basic position. Thus, in an attempt to tidy
up the 'shanty town' which Toye puts forward, some writers have suggested an 'urban renewal programme' where sufficiently similar
theories are housed together. Like all such 'slum clearance programmes', these ideas have attracted their critics. One of the earliest
attempts to find a way of classifying learning theories, was the work of
Kingsley and Garry in 1957, who suggested that all these theories might
be classified either as (1) Association or Stimulus-Response (represented by Thorndike, Guthrie and Hull) or (2) Field Theories (Lewin,
Tolman and the Gestalt Psychologists). (Kingsley and Garry 1957 p 83)
Not content with this, Taba in 1962, expanded the groups to form (1)
Associationist or Behaviourist theories, and (2) Organismic, Gestalt
and Field Theories. (Taba 1962 p 80)

In 1964, McDonald identified six major streams of theory, and in their seminal work on Theories of Learning, Hilgard and Bower reviewed the work of learning researchers under eleven categories:

Thorndike's Connectionism
Pavlov's Classical Conditioning
Guthrie's Contiguous Conditioning
Skinner's Operant Conditioning
Hull's Systematic Behaviour Theory
Tolman's Sign Learning
Gestalt Theory
Freud's Psychodynamics
Functionalism
Mathematical Learning Theory
Information Processing Models.

These, they said, really fall into two major families, (1) Stimulus-Response Theories, and (2) Cognitive Theories (Hilgard and Bower 1966 p 8). They did not consider the Humanistic Psychologies (Maslow, Rogers etc.) which are sometimes called 'Third Force' Psychologies.

In 1970, Reese and Overton offered a particularly innovative way of looking at the problem. They started off with the proposition that

Any theory presupposes a more general model according to which the theoretical concepts are formulated.
(Reese and Overton, 1970, p 117)

This idea is echoed in Bigge's analysis of Learning Theories for Teachers when he writes:

Each major learning theory school is representative of a broader and more or less comprehensive psychological system or basic outlook. Furthermore, each view of the learning process implies an outlook in regard to the nature and source of human motivation...
(Bigge, 1971, p 14)

Reese and Overton, then, suggested two world views or metaphysical systems, which constitute basic models of the essential characteristics of man and indeed of the nature of reality. The two systems are the mechanistic world view, which regards the Universe as machinelike, predictable and quantifiable, and sees man as passive, empty, and robot-like; and the organismic model, which regards both man and the

Universe as essentially active rather than static, and as being in a constant state of development and transformation.

When it is recognised that Theories of Learning inevitably reflect one or the other of these views, and that a compromise is logically impossible, it becomes clear that learning theory (and psychology generally) is still in what Kuhn (1970) calls the pre-paradigm phase, and it is hardly surprising that research in the natural science mould has been less than successful.

Theory from Practice

It is widely acknowledged that teaching is neither a random, nor a purposeless activity. Furthermore, whether aware of it or not,

> every mentor has a philosophy of education. He may not call it such a pretentious label, but he has some purpose in teaching as he does. A philosophy of education is a statement of the values, purposes and reasons for the entire educational enterprise.
>
> (Pittenger and Gooding, 1971, p 3)

It therefore follows that one logical direction of educational research is to attempt to discover, either by direct elicitation, or by observation (or some combination of the two), the assumptions and principles which underlie the practices of effective teachers. There are, however, manifold problems with both approaches.

Direct Elicitation

The greatest problem here is that, for various reasons, an effective practitioner may be unable (or unwilling) to verbalise his/her 'theory of teaching', or for that matter, to identify the components of professional effectiveness. Though other thinkers and writers have pointed out this phenomenon, Argyris and Schön have isolated the very useful distinction between 'theory in use' and 'espoused theory'. Like many others, * they start off with the fundamental premise that theory does

---

*   A sample statement: Any sharp distinction between theoretical, imaginative knowledge, and the action that stems from such knowledge is faulty. Action, whether part of teaching or any other activity in life, either is linked with theory, or it is blind and purposeless. Consequently, any purposeful action is governed by theory. (Bigge 1971 p 5)

underlie all deliberate behaviour, but then go on to say:

> When someone is asked how he would behave under certain
> circumstances, the answer he usually gives is his espoused
> theory of action for that particular situation. This is the theory
> of action to which he gives allegiance and which, upon request,
> he communicates to others. However, the theory that actually
> governs his actions is his theory-in-use, which may or may not
> be compatible with his espoused theory; furthermore, the indi-
> vidual may or may not be aware of the incompatibility of the
> two theories.
>
> (Argyris and Schön, 1974, pp 6/7)

So here we have the idea of a private theory and a public one, with the
distinct possibility of a discrepancy between the two. It is apparent that
a teacher might have a carefully elaborated and internally consistent
'espoused theory', and at the same time be guided by quite a different
theory-in-use.

Observation

In trying to find out what someone's theory-in-use is, there is little
point in asking them, because (by definition) all we will get is their
espoused theory. If we want to know what really 'makes someone tick',
then

> We must construct his theory-in-use from observations of his
> behaviour. In this sense, constructs of theories-in-use are like
> scientific hypotheses, the constructs may be inaccurate repre-
> sentations of the behaviour they claim to describe.
>
> (Argyris and Schön, 1974, p 7)

This process of inferring, however, is easier said than done:

> Inferring explicit theories of action from observed behaviour has
> (immense) problems. The task is to devise progressively more
> adequate constructions of theories-in-use that account for regu-
> larities of behaviour, deviations due to external or internal
> inhibitions, and behavioural manifestations of inconsistent
> theories-in-use.
>
> (Argyris and Schön, 1974, p 11)

Notwithstanding such difficulties, the observation of 'master teachers'
is a time-honoured practice, and has become something of a specialised
field of study in its own right.

Observation plays its proper role in research on teacher effect-
tiveness, when an attempt is made to gain insight into the nature
of effective teaching. Some understanding of the nature of effective teaching would seem to be a prerequisite to effective preparation of teachers, because of the clues it could afford as to
what they should be taught, i. e. as to the repertory of behaviours
an effective teacher must possess

(Medley and Mitzel, 1963, p 249)

This rests on the often implicit assumption that manifest behaviour is
somehow linked to purpose, or theory:

We can observe deliberate behaviour and try to account for it
as though it were the behaviour of fish or tides... (or) we can
regard deliberate human behaviour as the consequence of
theories of action held by humans, in which case we explain or
predict a person's behaviour by attributing to him a theory of
action.

(Argyris and Schön, 1974, p 5)

In other words, by watching how a teacher behaves in a classroom, we
can make certain inferences about that teacher's 'theory of teaching',
and hence derive, inductively, a theoretical model, upon which to build
a pattern of generalised teaching competencies.

Since the behaviour of teachers only has real meaning in the context of
interacting with learners, the major trend has been towards the simul-
taneous observation of both teacher and students. In fact, the spontane-
ous cut and thrust of classroom interaction is likely to reveal more
about the teacher's 'true' theory, than his/her performance in a carefully rehearsed, planned and orchestrated presentation, where learners
may scarcely impinge at all:

If a pupil asks a question that seems irrelevant there may be
five or ten seconds in which to respond. Is the question a serious
indication of an important misunderstanding? Is there time to
digress, and would it be worthwhile? What would he, and other
pupils, learn from such a digression, or from a refusal to digress? Is it, on the other hand, a flippant attempt to embarrass
the teacher, and if so why was it made? What are the other
pupils' attitudes to this pupil? Is there a way of turning the
question to useful educational purposes?

Of course there is not time to work rationally through such a complex of choices. The teacher responds intuitively. His response is influenced by assessments he makes, or fails to make, on all those questions.

(Sutton, 1975, pp 336/7)

One of the major difficulties of classroom observation therefore, is that

classroom behaviour is so complicated, occurs on so many levels, so rapidly, and with so many individuals, that a representation of even a small part of the events is difficult.

(Morrison and McIntyre, 1969, p 28)

This has been noted by both Jackson (1968) and Adams and Biddle (1970) who suggest that the number of discriminable acts, utterances, or sentences spoken by classroom participants may be in the thousands for a given lesson.

(Dunkin and Biddle, 1974, p 58)

Some sort of mechanism needs to be employed to reduce either the speed or the complexity of the events being observed. One technique developed to cope with this problem, was the post-session rating schedule (for example Ryans' Teacher Characteristic Schedule), whereby the observer sits in the classroom observing specific areas of behaviour covered by the schedule, and at the end goes away and attempts to distil his observations into a number of ratings. There are, however, limitations with such a technique and, as Dunkin and Biddle point out

Many investigators are now taking advantage of such technological tools as audio and video tape recorders to make stabilized records of the teaching process, that can be studied at leisure.

(Dunkin and Biddle, 1974, p 58)

Whilst it might be academically interesting for researchers to compute what proportion of time is taken up by the teacher, or to analyse in great detail a particular exchange between teacher and taught, such enquiries have a curious habit of becoming ends in themselves, and researchers often can lose sight of the fact that teachers have to handle situations as they occur and cannot afford the luxury of lengthy contemplation, analysis and introspection.

Most of (the drawbacks of live observation) stem from the complexity and rapid pace of classroom events... As an example of this, the reader might try to keep track of the exact sequence of speakers (using a checklist of the names of all persons in a given classroom) during a classroom lesson. Even when he is trained and uses a number or letter code for each pupil, the reader will probably have difficulty with the task. Now try to code each utterance for its warmth, wit or wisdom!

(Dunkin and Biddle, 1974, p 61)

This is just the tip of the iceberg. Even if verbal interactions did represent the sum total of classroom behaviour, there would be the problems of ulterior or hidden dimensions to apparently straightforward exchanges (see, for instance, Duff, 1972). But in fact there are countless subtle nuances in any classroom situation, and the simple fact is that no observation instrument yet developed can come anywhere near monitoring every dimension in the classroom situation. Supporters of observation (like Medley and Mitzel) would argue, however, that even distorted and incomplete data about teaching, is better than none.

To make matters worse, there is a logical perplexity inherent in designing instruments to assist classroom observation. I have already shown that it is flatly impossible to observe and record everything which happens in the classroom, in fact it would be pointless to try, because

if all behaviour were to be accounted for, the resulting account would be so complex that it would not help us to understand and guide behaviour.

(Agryris and Schön, 1974, p 37)

The researcher is therefore obliged to select those dimensions which he anticipates will reveal the most useful data.

A scientist's inventions assist him in two ways: they tell him what to expect and they help him to see it when it happens. Those that tell him what to expect are theoretical inventions and those that enable him to observe outcomes are instrumental inventions. The two types are never wholly independent of each other, and they usually stem from the same assumptions. This is unavoidable. Moreover, without his inventions, both theoretical and instrumental, man would be both disoriented and blind. He would not know where to look, or how to see.

(Kelly, 1969, p 94)

Thus, researchers are likely to focus on those behaviours which they expect to reveal important and useful information about teacher effectiveness, and perhaps overlook unexpected dimensions which are, in fact, more significant.

Even if we could overcome the manifold problems of adequate observation, and of somehow reconstructing the theory-in-use relevant to a particular instance of behaviour,

> Theories-in-use do all include assumptions about self, others, the situation, and the connections among action, consequence and situation... Theories-in-use include knowledge about the behaviour of physical objects, the making and use of artifacts, the market place, organisations, and every other domain of human activity. In other words, the full set of assumptions about human behaviour that function in theories-in-use constitute a psychology of everyday life.
>
> (Argyris and Schön, 1974, pp 7/8)

The problems of attempting to elicit an individual practitioner's theories-in-use are made even more complex, when we acknowledge that they are hierarchically ordered, thus leading to the possibility that some event or circumstance may act as a 'trigger', invoking an altogether different theory-in-use. Argyris and Schön explain it this way:

> Each person has many theories-in-use, one for every kind of situation in which he more or less regularly finds himself. We will call each of these a microtheory, although each person's theories-in-use are not independent atoms of theory. One's microtheories are related to one another through similarities of content and through their logic. As with any complex body of knowledge, a person's theories-in-use may be organised in a variety of ways...
>
> A person often holds different and incompatible theories-in-use for situations that appear to an outside observer to be alike. (For instance) he may be said to have a higher order theory that governs his use of different subtheories-in-use according to (differences which he perceives in the situation).
>
> (Argyris and Schön, 1974, pp 8/9)

The whole business of trying to infer exactly which theoretical convictions and assumptions underlie even one tiny piece of overt behaviour is an enormous gamble, attempts to elucidate an entire educational philosophy based on observation, confront almost insurmountable difficulties. It is hardly surprising, (though nevertheless disappointing) to find, therefore, that although over 10, 000 published studies have appeared (Dunkin and Biddle, 1974, p 12)

> no universally 'good' patterns have emerged. Despite the tire-less efforts of several investigators to identify classroom styles which might be shown to produce consistent gains in learning, improvements in (learners') attitudes to school, or high efficiency ratings from observers, little has emerged.
> (Wragg, 1974, p 71)

Indeed, Knowles has described the search for objective and quantifiable characteristics which distinguish excellent from mediocre teachers as 'one of the more or less futile quests of educational researchers over the years.' (Knowles, 1973, p 89)

Integrating Theory into Practice

In addition to the immense philosophical and methodological problems which have beset these two systems of deriving theoretical frameworks for trainee teachers, other researchers and teacher educators have begun to question the very idea of whether or not student teachers are given enough help in making the transition successfully from theory into practice. Whilst, for instance, it could be argued as a distinct advantage that courses in educational theory

> do not make explicit the processes by which teachers might provide optimal conditions for learning in the classroom,
> (Dunkin and Biddle, 1974, p 21)

others have argued the other way, namely that:

> teachers need to know how (learners) learn and how they depend on motivation, readiness and reinforcement. But... teachers similarly need to know how to teach - how to motivate pupils, assess their readiness, act on the assessment, present the sub-ject, maintain discipline, and shape a cognitive structure. Too much of educational psychology makes the teacher infer what he needs to do from what he is told about learners and learning. Theories of teaching would make explicit how teachers behave, why they behave as they do, and with what effects.
> (Gage, 1963, p 133)

It certainly seems, at least early in their teaching careers, that teachers do not have the time, or the inclination to map out a teaching strategy based on their knowledge of educational theory because

> the student teacher is too desperately immersed in the intoxicating task of survival to stop and deliberate how these zealously acquired concepts might affect his classroom behaviour.
>
> (Wragg, 1974, p vii)

Indeed, this assertion is supported by the 1964 findings of Joyce and Harootunian, which I mentioned in Chapter One.

> (The investigators) questioned student teachers on teaching practice to discover how they determined their objectives, planned their lessons etc. They concluded that nearly all the decision making processes had little to do with rational educational theory. Lessons rarely had objectives, and methods were intuitively arrived at, and were not chosen from alternatives. Most lessons were reflections of the co-operating teacher and of practice in the teaching practice school. The writers inferred from their observations that students tended to borrow the practices they saw, rather than create original tactics.
>
> (Joyce and Harootunian, 1964, cit Wragg, 1974, p 63)

However, the period of teaching practice is acknowledged to be one of great pressure and intensity, and we might expect that, within a couple of years, a new teacher would exhibit an appropriate blend of confidence and enthusiasm, to develop a comprehensive repertoire of teaching behaviour. Unfortunately, however, this does not seem necessarily to be the case. Other researchers have shown that teaching styles are remarkably stable, and that there is generally very little tendency to change teaching styles and patterns after the period of initial teaching practice. It would appear, therefore, that many teachers simply do not make the sort of conscious, considered and careful teaching decisions which this model of teacher education presupposes. This conclusion, regrettably, is confirmed by Clark and Nisbet's follow-up of Scottish teachers, two years after graduating:

> Reacting to their training course, these teachers, especially the graduates, reported that teaching practice had been the most useful part of the course. The writers observed that the students questioned saw their training primarily as a matter of learning techniques, and regarded many other things as a waste of time.
>
> (Clark and Nisbet in Wragg, 1974, pp 67-8, Underlining mine)

Thus research evidence tends to suggest that merely exposing students to the results of studies of teaching and learning is insufficient, per se, for them to develop an appropriate range of teaching strategies.

SUMMARY

Where does all this leave us? The argument so far may be summarised as follows. The emergence of teaching as a profession is linked to, and indeed dependent upon, attempts to identify the theories which underlie it. Likewise, the training of teachers has tended to become increasingly 'theoretical' in an attempt to improve the quality of teaching practice. Whilst many enquiries into learning have elucidated particular aspects of how things are learned, most 'theories of learning' are aggregations of findings, rather than general laws - they certainly leave something to be desired as unambiguous guides to action, for teachers. Similarly, attempts to discover what it is about 'master teachers' which makes them particularly effective have been fraught with difficulties. Gage (1972, p 38) lists four characteristics which do seem to be supported by most research findings - warmth, indirectness, cognitive organisation and enthusiasm. There are, however, plenty of difficulties in turning such generalisations into competencies which can be quantified, measured and taught to new teachers! In both cases, there is evidence to suggest that trainee teachers often fail to integrate these research findings effectively into their existing 'frames of reference'. As Mulford observes:

> New information and skills must be rooted in continuing education experiences which also allow examination of one's cognitive, moral and ethical frames of reference. These predispositions determine whether and how these skills and knowledge will eventually be utilized.
>
> (Mulford, 1979, p 163)

In this statement, we may be getting closer to an understanding of the problem which has confronted teacher educators - namely that of integrating theory and practice at the individual or personal level. In fact there is, writes Francis,

> a widespread misconception of the nature of educational theory, Such a misconception equates theory with idealistic, impractical bookbound stuff, and equates academic with pointless. Student antipathy and teacher antipathy towards educational theory stems from this misconception. It is therefore important, if integration

of theory and practice is our aim, that educational theory comes to be seen not so much as a corpus of knowledge informed by contributing disciplines - history, philosophy, psychology etc, - but rather as an activity, the activity of <u>critical reflection</u>. This activity, <u>theorizing</u>, should draw upon the body of knowledge which is the product of former, prominent theorists, but yet should <u>subordinate this knowledge to the reflection upon the current professional experience of the student teacher. The most important theorizer in a teacher education programme is not Plato, Rogers or Britton; the most important theorizer is the student himself</u>.

(Francis, 1980, p 17, Underlining mine)

CONCLUSION

In this Chapter, I have focussed on two contentious areas of teacher education - firstly the question of 'natural' teaching style, and secondly the perennial problem of linking theory and practice. In both cases, I have argued, the effectiveness of specific programmes has been limited by a failure to take account of the student teachers' "cognitive, moral and ethical frames of reference". The predominant paradigm within which teacher education generally has proceeded, has been subject-centred and instructor-dominated. In the remainder of this monograph, I will discuss a technique which, I believe, has the potential to overcome, at least in part, this failure to account adequately for the student teacher's perspective.

CHAPTER III

PERSONAL CONSTRUCT THEORY AND REPERTORY GRID TECHNIQUE

PERSONAL CONSTRUCT THEORY

> If we can accept that (people) have two important basic attributes - an innate and powerful drive to relate to others, and a continuing attempt to make sense of their experiences - then we can see that failure to satisfy the first drive may result from failure in the second area, that is to say from incomplete or distorted modes of making sense of the self and others. It is for this reason that the study of the concepts (people) hold of themselves and others, and the clarification of how they succeed or fail in communicating with each other, is of central psychological interest....
>
> (Ryle, 1975, pp 1/2)

For centuries, philosophers have debated whether or not there is an objective reality which, though we may not be able to see it yet, will one day be fully revealed. The recent advances of science, far from solving this dilemma have, if anything, intensified it (see, for instance, Polanyi) and in recent years there has been increasing emphasis on individual structures of meaning or, to paraphrase Berger and Luckman, personally constructed realities. This relativity of knowledge has influenced many fields, and the certainty and absoluteness which characterised many disciplines until fairly recently, has given way to a univeral and pervasive tentativeness, ambivalence and uncertainty which seems to characterise this last half of the twentieth century.

> From physics to sociology, there has been a general awakening to the relativity of all knowing and the implications of this for how man may handle the realities which he constructs. Heisenberg showed the impossibility of measuring the complete system of an entity accurately. Einstein constructed a universe in which even the basic dimensions of time, space and energy depend upon the time, space and energy of the observer. Polanyi has explored the whole nature of the scientific enterprise in terms of the

integrity of the knowing of each individual scientist. Lorenz has progressively explored the realities of the members of species at different levels in the phylogenetic scale until he now sees man as one, probably unstable, attempt by living matter to reflect the nature of reality. Levi-Strauss in anthropology sees the very patterns of man's thoughts and feelings as competent reactions to the challenge of living in the cultural, natural and technological settings in which he is placed. Herbert Mead and Schutz see reality as a social construction which receives much of its individual validation from transactions with other people who share it.

(Thomas, 1978, p 49)

According to Thomas, "George Kelly has expressed this general paradigm for psychology within personal construct theory". In other words, Kelly offers a psychology whose very essence lies in the different ways in which individuals make sense of what happens to them. Kelly expresses it in these terms:

Man looks at his world through transparent patterns or templets which he creates and then attempts to fit over the realities of which the world is composed. The fit is not always very good. Yet without such patterns the world appears to be such an undifferentiated homogeneity that man is unable to make any sense out of it. Even a poor fit is more helpful to him than nothing at all.

(Kelly, 1955, p 8-9)

If this basic notion is accepted, several questions present themselves - what form do these patterns or templets take, how are they arrived at, how do they influence behaviour, to what extent are they shared by society at large and can they be changed? These, and many other questions, are addressed by Kelly in his two volume Psychology of Personal Constructs, published in 1955, and in subsequent writings, both by Kelly and by others.

Kelly chooses to call these patterns 'constructs'. He states that they are sometimes explicitly formulated and other times implicitly acted out, they may be verbally expressed or utterly inarticulate, consistent with other courses of behaviour or inconsistent with them, intellectually reasoned, or intuitively sensed. (Kelly, 1955, p 9). The critical factor about these constructs is that they simultaneously allow people to make sense of reality, and at the same time limit their possible alternative interpretations. A simple example may help. If you are lost in an unfamiliar city, expecially one where the language is foreign, you might decide by reference to your pocket map that you are at a certain intersection. You glance around for confirming evidence - yes, over there is an entrance to the subway; up that road there seems to be a church; there certainly was a small park just a few hundred yards away. You decide that the Art Gallery you are seeking is only just around the corner... It isn't of course! You have been looking at another part of the map, ignoring the conflicting or inconsistent evidence (like the fact that you should be able to see a bridge, or something) concentrating instead only on the items of information which seem to fit.

To extend this metaphor of maps a little further, it is as if each person had created a representational model of reality inside his or her head, and then proceeded to navigate a way through life using this individual map or model. The model will only be altered if it is found to be wanting; so long as it serves as an adequate guide, it will continue in use the way it is.

This focuses attention on the problem of communication. Have you ever had the experience of someone explaining to you, perhaps over the telephone, the layout of a building, or the directions for finding some location? How often do you end up with a different 'mental image' from what it turns out to be really like? Ryle comments that "if the relationship between two people is likened to a voyage, then it is as if the two participants are using charts with the same titles, but with systematic differences of scale, shape and direction in respect of main features" (Ryle, 1975, p 2). He states:

> The communication we achieve with others is based on the fact that the meanings of the words gestures and symbolical actions we employ are, to an incomplete but adequate extent, shared. We are most sure of achieving communication when we are explicit about the language used, as for example, in formal logic or rigorous science, and we are most aware of communicating poorly when we lack a common language or where it is obvious that differences in experiences and culture are leading to differing interpretations of the language used. Between these extremes of clear, explicit communication and obviously imperfect communication, there lies a wide zone where more or less adequate understanding is achieved, but within which communication is impoverished or distorted to an extent, and in ways, that are not always apparent.

(Ryle, 1975, p 2)

This fact seems, to me, to have important implications for the enter- prise of teaching and learning. Above all, it seems to emphasize the absolute need to 'start from where the learner is' a counsel of perfec- tion for all but the 'born' teacher to do intuitively.

> The experienced teacher may be able to make informed guesses which work some of the time for some of the class, but there is a need for a simple technique for encouraging each learner to express his or her understanding of a topic or area in his or her own terms in a form which both the learner and the teacher or tutor can easily understand and use.
>
> (Shaw and Thomas, 1978, p 139)

It is argued that the Repertory Grid Technique, which is the subject of this monograph, provides just such a technique for exploring and 'externalizing' personal structures of meaning.

So far, I have given some sort of intuitive 'feel' for Kelly's Personal Constructs, but a more precise description is needed. According to Kelly, we build up our construct systems by participating in life, in fact he argues that one of mankind's distinguishing characteristics, is the ability to represent the environment, and that at any time we are free to revise an interpretation of the universe. To take a simple example, you may choose to represent and to treat all dogs as friendly animals. This choice in itself, is not an innate characteristic, it is a learned behaviour based on a series of past experiences. The construct friendly-unfriendly has no meaning in itself, it only has meaning when applied to living creatures, and it is essentially a personal and subjec- tive evaluation. After a succession of unfortunate incidents, you may choose to move some dogs (or maybe even all dogs) from one end of the continuum to the other. Your definition of friendly-unfriendly may remain the same, but you now see some creatures as occupying a dif- ferent position on the spectrum.

Alternatively, you may leave dogs classified as 'friendly' but introduce another construct to do with approachable-unapproachable. A third possibility would be to decide that friendly-unfriendly is really an in- appropriate construct to apply to dogs at all, and that whatever charact- eristics you would use in describing humans in this way simply do not fit with dogs - they lie outside the range of convenience of the construct. These few examples are in no way exhaustive of how our construct systems are shaped by events, they are simple examples. The point is that our construct systems are initiated and modified by interactions with the real world, and that they are subject to alteration in the healthy and fully functioning person, when they are found to lead to undesirable consequences.

In the above example, I have introduced the notion of bipolarity; a construct can best be described as a pathway, with destinations at either end:

> Each path can be viewed as a two-way street, and while the individual may choose either of these directions, he cannot, so to speak, strike out across country without building new constructions, new routes to follow.

> When a person must move, he is confronted by a series of dichotomous choices - each choice being channelled by a construct. Each construct represents a pair of rival hypotheses, either of which may be applied to a new element which the person seeks to construe. Thus, just as the experimental scientist designs his experiments around rival hypotheses, so each person is seen as designing his daily explorations of life around the rival hypotheses which are yielded by the constructs within his system. Moreover, just as the scientist cannot foresee possibilities that he has not, in some manner, conceptualised in terms of hypotheses, so any individual can prove or disprove only that which his construction system allows him to see in terms of possible alternatives, The construct system sets limits beyond which it is impossible for a person to perceive, and in this way constructs are seen as controls on a person's outlook and also, in an ultimate sense, as controls on his behaviour.

> (Bannister and Mair, 1968, p 27)

This scientific analogy is really central to Kelly's theory. Intrigued by the paradox that many psychological theories are themselves insufficiently complex to account for the creativity of their inventors, Kelly postulated that perhaps scientists were merely doing, in a specialised way, what people do as a matter of course. Kelly proposed the idea of 'man-as-scientist' or, in other words, a psychology based on the notion that we habitually seek to make sense out of reality in a systematic way, anticipating events according to our constructs, and constantly evaluating experience against the anticipations.

According to Kelly's theory, our construct systems are complex and intricate, consisting of an interdependent and hierarchical network, with subordinate constructs at the base, and increasingly abstract, superordinate constructs higher up.

These superordinate constructs are generally considered to be more resistant to change than the looser, and more permeable constructs lower down the system. If this point of view is accepted, it seems to have important implications for the practice of education. This is particularly true of teacher education where, as I have argued in Chapter 2, teaching is influenced by higher order concerns such as ideological assumptions, metaphorical models of the learning process, personal learning style and self concept. What is required is some sort of mechanism for exploring these tacit dimensions of people's construct systems, with a view to facilitating their change, and this is the province of the Repertory Grid Technique.

REPERTORY GRID TECHNIQUE

If you have followed the presentation thus far, it will come as no surprise to learn of Kelly's distaste for conventional psychological testing which, he argues, requires the respondent or subject to enter into the construct system of the experimenter, rather than vice versa. As a result, he devised an innovative and imaginative research methodology, which is consistent with the assumptions underlying his theory; its full title is Role Construct Repertory Test and Grid, which is often abbreviated to Reptest or RepGrid.

The repertory grid technique enables the elicitation and exploration of part of a person's construct system. This is particularly valuable in an educational context where the learner may be encouraged to explore some tacit and almost subconscious dimensions of his or her construct system as a preparation to some educational experience. To understand fully the method, it is best to look at Kelly's concept of constructs.

> Kelly offers several definitions of a construct. For example, a construct is a 'a way in which two or more things are alike, and thereby different from a third or more things...' His argument is that we never affirm anything without simultaneously denying something... We do not always, or even very often, specify our contrast pole, but Kelly's argument is that we make sense out of our world by simultaneously noting likenesses and differences.

It is in the contrast that the usefulness of the construct subsists.
(Fransella and Bannister, 1977, p 5)

Kelly argued that if a person were presented with any three items out
of an array and asked to group them in such a way that two of the items
were similar to each other and the third one dissimilar along the same
mode of discrimination, then we would be able to discover a construct
that the person characteristically uses in evaluating events in the world.
If this procedure were repeated with a number of groups of three items,
and each time the respondent was encouraged to identify a different and
significant way of distinguishing the items, bit by bit it would be possible to build up some sort of model of the constructs which that person
uses in evaluating events, ideas, or people in their life. An example
might help here. If I present you with the names of three cities - say
London, Tokyo and Sydney, and ask you to say in what way two of them
are similar, and different to the third, you might group them like this -

        London - Sydney   :   English Speaking
        Tokyo   :   Non-English Speaking

It would then be possible for you to use this construct as a way of
distinguishing other cities, say Madrid, New York, and Rio de Janeiro.
Alternatively, you might say -

        London - Tokyo   :   Northern Hemisphere
        Sydney   :   Southern Hemisphere

and again you could use this distinction to classify other cities. If I did
this a number of times, each time presenting you with three different
cities, you might come up with a number of constructs such as size,
importance, cost of housing, temperature, even 'pleasantness', and so
on. These constructs could then be applied to a much wider range of
cities than just the three used in the elicitation.

There are many variations and sophistications of this arrangement -
the triads may be selected purposely or randomly; one element may be
held constant in each group; the subject may be asked to supply his or
her own elements, or at least to supplement those provided by the
experimenter; sometimes more or less than three elements may be
offered to the subject; the elements may be verbal or non-verbal (for
instance, items of sculpture); the experimenter may only ask for a term
to describe one end of the bipolar construct and leave the other end
'submerged'; the respondent may be asked to indicate and define opposite

ends of the constructs without using words; and in some research work
the researcher has even supplied and constructs, merely asking subjects
to rank the elements, though I cannot help feeling that this is getting
away somewhat from Kelly's original concept of the investigator getting
inside the respondent's construct system, rather than vice versa.
(Adams-Webber, 1970).

Whatever,the approach, the idea is usually to present the subject with a
series of different stimuli, intended to trigger a different construct in
each case. This procedure, in a more or less elaborate form, yields
a matrix or grid, where the elements comprise one dimension or axis,
and the constructs the other. Once these constructs have been elicited
from a subject, it is then possible to ask the subject to rank or rate all
the elements in the array (not just those used to elicit that particular
construct) along the continuum thus identified. If this procedure is
undertaken a number of times, say 12 or 15 times, and using an
original listing of 12 or 15 elements in the array, it is possible to produce quite a valuable insight into part of the person's construct system
in the form of a matrix of numbers. The numerical data obtained in
this way,

> can be subject to many of the kinds of group statistics which we
> have hitherto reserved for populations of subjects. Cluster
> analysis methods, t-tests of group differences, correlational
> consistency measures, significance of correlation methods,
> co-efficients of concordance and a range of other measures are
> technically feasible.
>
> (Fransella and Bannister, 1977, p 9)

It may be possible to discover which constructs are superordinate and
which are subordinate, to combine constructs into clusters or to identify
underlying components which seem to account for a certain proportion
of the variance in the total grid, to calculate distances and angles
between various constructs and elements, and even to plot them onto
'cognitive maps'. But a Repertory Grid is much more than a research
tool, for it has been shown that the act of completing a grid can be, in
itself, a valuable learning experience. This potential for learning may
be increased if 'self' is used as one of the elements in the original
array.

> Kelly suggests that the controlling influence of constructs
> becomes particularly interesting when a person begins to use
> himself as an event in the context of the constructs he is develop-
> ing or operating. When a person uses himself as a datum in

forming new constructs, he finds that the constructs formed operate as a tight control on his own behaviour. In forming a set of constructs which include the self as an element within their range of convenience, the person plots the dimensions along which it will be possible to organise his own behaviour in relation to others. Thus a person who includes himself in the context of the construct say, powerful - weak, binds himself to assess his own behaviour in relation to that dimension. Whether he sees himself as powerful or weak is of interest to the psychologist, but it is secondary to the fact that the person has ordered his world and himself with respect to the powerful-weak dimension.

(Bannister and Mair, 1968, pp 27-8)

CONCLUSION

Though Kelly first developed his theory and his Reptest for psychotherapeutic applications, practitioners in many other fields have been stimulated by the promise of its more general applicability, and a quick review of the literature reveals its imaginative use in a variety of fields. These include: studies of self-concept and weight loss, sociability and interpersonal effectiveness, stutterers' construing of speaking, promoting reading skills, political preferences and voting patterns, personal structures of meaning and 'learning to learn', colour preferences and comprehending map formats, and architects' construing of space. Glanville shows the immense potential of Repertory Grid Technique in Art Education, and Boot and Boxer, working at the London Business School, have developed innovative approaches to the development of managers using a modified Repertory Grid in an interactive computer programme. Several researchers have explored the usefulness of the technique in the professional development of Social Work students (Lifshitz, 1974 and Rytovaara, 1979), and or agricultural extension officers (Salmon, 1979). It is hardly surprising to find that a few researchers have recognised the potential of Personal Construct Theory in Teacher Training, and it is this application to which I will now turn.

CHAPTER IV

PERSONAL CONSTRUCTS AND THE TRAINING OF TEACHERS

According to Brundage and MacKeracher, two conflicting assumptions
may be found in the training of teachers;

- The first assumption suggests that all teachers should follow
  the same learning program, since all are alike in role tasks
  and needs, and that these standardised programs can be
  implemented either through group processes or through individual learning modules.

- The second assumption suggests that each teacher should be
  able to design his own individualized self-directed learning
  program, especially tailored to his personal learning needs,
  and that this program can only be implemented through individual and independent activities.
                          (Brundage and MacKeracher, 1980, p 90)

They go on to say that both assumptions appear to be valid within
certain limits and conclude with the comment that "the most pragmatic
approach to teacher training involves some combination of large-group
work, small-group work, and individual activities based on both individual and group learning needs". (p 91)

If the arguments presented earlier in this monograph, concerning
natural teaching style and the relationship between theory and practice,
are accepted, it should be apparent that my contention is that natural
teaching style is a behavioural manifestation of individual beliefs about
teaching (theories in use), and that the appropriate place to begin with
the development of teachers is with their more or less well-formed
constructs about teaching.

To some extent, the importance of these orientations has been
implicitly acknowledged in the unending succession of studies aimed at
assessing the attitudes and personal values of student teachers and
teachers-in-service. In 1958, for instance, Runkel suggested that the
'frames of reference' of the teacher were a significant determinant of

classroom behaviour, and in the years since then, many other researchers and theorists have emphasised the central importance of personal
philosophies, or individual structures of meaning in training professionals. Argyris and Schön, for instance, write

> ... each person lives in a behavioural world of his own - a
> world made up of his own behaviour in interaction with the
> behaviour of others. Each person's behavioural world is there-
> fore artificial not only in the sense that it consists of artifacts
> of human conviction, but in the sense that it is shaped and
> influenced by one's own action and by one's theories of the
> behavioural world as they influence action. The relationship
> between theory-in-use and action is special. Here the action
> not only applies and tests the theory, but also shapes the
> behavioural world the theory is about. We are familiar with this
> phenomenon in its pejorative connotations, as in the example of
> the teacher whose belief in the stupidity of his students results
> in the students' behaving stupidly. But the usual conclusion of
> such experiments is that one should avoid self-fulfilling
> prophecies - as if one could. Every theory-in-use is a self-
> fulfilling prophecy to some extent.
>
> (Argyris and Schön, 1974, pp 17-18)

Brundage and MacKeracher, quoting the work of Ireland et al, and of
Hunt, write:

> Teachers are more likely to utilize organising principles which
> they have developed for themselves through reflecting on their
> own personal experience. This process could be described as
> 'personal-experience - into personal constructs - into
> practice'...
>
> Hunt argues that the teacher must be able to function as a linking
> agent whose personal experience, meanings, and organizing
> principles provide the basis for building connections between
> theory and practice. This view suggests that learning programs
> should focus more on assisting teacher learners to develop their
> own constructs, organizing principles and strategies for teach-
> ing than on presenting the constructs of remote theorists.
>
> (Brundage and MacKeracher, 1980, p 30)

The same theme is evident in the writings of Thomas and Harri-
Augstein:

The learner almost certainly values changes in both his experience and his actions which the teacher thinks of less highly.

Thus, for the authors, the construct:

As viewed by the teacher

v

As viewed by the learner

is an important differentiation to be made in thinking and feeling about learning.

The point of view of the teacher (or of the experimenter in psychological learning experiments) pervades the literature on learning. It also colours the thoughts and feelings of most individuals who have been through school, college or university. Most of the supposed theories of learning are solely concerned with the conditions under which teacher-defined learning takes place and methods for enhancing the purposes of the teacher. They are thus theories of teaching. It is only when the purposes of the learner are used as a basis for assessing what learning has taken place that an approach can be made to understanding the individual processes of learning. Earlier it was suggested that learner-defined learning could be viewed as: "The construction and exchange of personally significant meaning"...

The construction of meaning may not be totally intentional. Many retrospectively valued changes take place unplanned by either an outside agency or the learner himself.

Thus another important dimension for construing learning is:

As assessed against the original purpose (if any)

v

As assessed retrospectively.

The two-by-two category system yielded by our two constructs serves as a useful device for clarifying thinking on this topic.

	Original purpose	Retrospective assessment
Teacher's view	Teacher original (TO)	Teacher retrospective (TR)
Learner's view	Learner original (LO)	Learner retrospective (LR)

Most learning in education falls into the TO-category. The teacher sets the purpose of the exercise and the learning is measured by reference to what he set out to teach.

Most personally valued learning falls into category LR. The learner recognizes after the event that something significant has happened. Then and only then does the learner set about evaluating what has happened...

Within a learner-centred personal construing approach to learning, type TO becomes irrelevant, except as a short-term exercise. Effective long-term learning is not achieved if the learner indiscriminately takes on someone else's meanings...
                    (Thomas and Harri-Augstein, 1977, pp 92-6)

Acknowledging the 'perspective of the personal' (Morris, 1972), a number of teacher educators have recognised the unique potential of Kelly's Theory of Personal Constructs, and in particular, his Repertory Grid Technique, as frameworks to facilitate the professional development of teachers. In 1974, Cove, in a paper entitled "A View of Teacher Self Evaluation", wrote:

Some interesting insights into possible ways of encouraging the process of teachers learning more and becoming more aware of themselves and of the (learners) and begin to act in accordance with what they learn, can be found in the work of George Kelly. Kelly evolved a theory of 'personal constructs' around the idea that man reacts to ideas in an individual way and puts them together in his own way and, hence, creates his own 'personal constructs' of reality. Kelly asks:

I wonder if we might not develop the notion of man as a society composed of 'empathic man' or 'inquiring man'. Men who seem to understand and do it by

active inquiry, using their own behaviour not as
something to act out, but as a means of understanding their world.

(Bannister and Fransella, 1971, p 50)

Kelly's suggestions lead to situations in which teachers investi-
gate themselves and their own classrooms at the same time.
This recognizes the situation that the teacher and the classroom
are an interacting entity and that if any change is to occur the
total situation must be examined and assessed by the teacher
himself. On the basis of the conclusions reached by the teacher,
change may be introduced and the result re-examined and acted
upon still further.

For example, the traditional method of providing assistance for
a teacher wishing to develop an open classroom situation would
be to provide some lectures or seminars or small group sessions
on the subject and to arrange some visits to see open classrooms.
The Kelly proposal as it is being developed by Peter Cameron in
a number of Tasmanian schools, uses as an essential preliminary measure, a method of assisting teachers to identify the
social values that unconsciously influence them in their work
and then involve them in working out alternative processes that
would lead to a better alignment of consciously modified beliefs
and action. The working out of this idea does not require the
intrusion of someone else into the private world of the classroom,
since the teacher can proceed to change himself in his own way,
if that is what he wants to do.

(Cove, 1974, p 14)

Working independently, but clearly within the same conceptual paradigm,
Pope (1978) conducted a research project to assess how student teachers
view the role of teaching, and how these perceptions alter during the
period of intensive teaching practice. She commences with the statement that "the 'frame of reference' of the student teacher is an important factor in his teaching behaviour. It would seem, therefore, that this
is an aspect that needs to be monitored and that the student teacher could
benefit from reflecting on the way he/she construes teaching". (Pope,
1978, p 77). The results of this project are reported more fully in her
paper on Teacher Training in Fransella (1978, op.cit.) but may be
summarised briefly as follows:

Volunteer subjects within two teacher training establishments were obtained and then randomly assigned to one of three groups:

Group 1 - Subjects interviewed before and after teaching practice.

Group 2 - Subjects interviewed before and after teaching practice, plus completion of three grids, one before, one during, and one on return to college after teaching practice.

Group 3 - Subjects completed the same schedule as Group 2, with the addition of feedback sessions, during which the analysis of their previous grid was discussed.

(Pope, 1978, p 77)

Each subject who completed a grid, provided his/her own elements, which were things the subject thought of when he/she had 'teaching' in mind. They were then presented with triads selected from the elements they had provided, and constructs elicited in the usual way. The grids produced were subjected to computer analysis by a programme called FOCUS (see Shaw, 1978, p 62) which, amongst other things, produces hierarchical element trees or cluster diagrams which, to quote Shaw, is a "method devised mainly for use in feeding back the analysis of the grid to the subject without displaying any mathematical 'magic', complex computer printout, or general problems of naming factors or components". (Shaw, 1978, p 62)

In addition to producing some intrinsically interesting data about how student teachers generally view teaching:

This case study illustrates that using grid analysis as a base, one can gain a great deal of insight into how the person feels about teaching in his/her own terms. I would suggest that these extracts tap issues of personal importance to the student teacher which will have significant bearing on both her performance as a teacher and her own career choice....

Having had some subjects complete grids without feedback, I was able to assess how useful I felt both methods were. I believe that the majority of subjects in Groups 2 and 3 enjoyed reflecting on their thoughts about teaching - many reported that it was probably the first time that they had sat back and reflected on their personal approach.

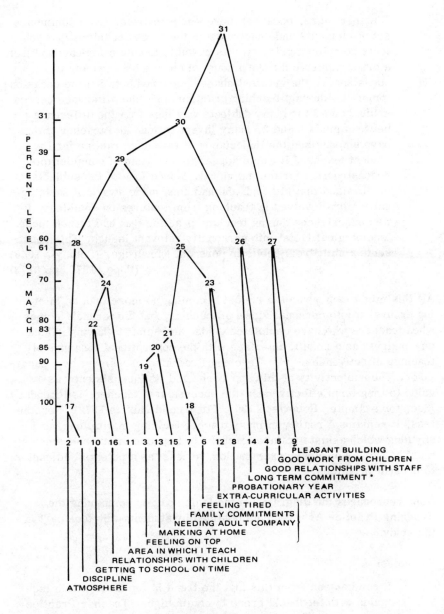

Element tree for grid completed during teaching practice.

(Pope, 1978 Reproduced by Permission Academic Press Inc. (London) Ltd)

(Further more, because) there was a (more or less) common
set of elements and constructs on the three occasions that subjects completed grids, it was possible to obtain for each subject,
a crude numeric for the amount of change between any two
occasions... the greatest change occurred between the occasions
'prior' to 'during' teaching practice since the difference between
grids 2 and 3 for many subjects was less than the difference
between grids 1 and 2. Many investigations into teacher training
have emphasized the importance of teaching practice for the
student teacher. It would appear to be a time of considerable
reconstruction for the individual. Indeed (one of the subjects)
emphasized that although she had been made aware of sociological factors involved in teaching from lectures on sociology, it
was experiences during teaching practice that had turned these
'sociological facts' into personally relevant issues. This represents a shift from public to personal knowledge. (Polanyi, 1958)

(Pope, 1978, pp 82/3)

All this might easily run the risk of becoming no more than an interesting excursion into personal views of teaching, but the 'crunch' comes
when teachers who have completed grids, and admit to having gained
new insights as a result, interface with the conventional measure of
teaching effectiveness - viz: Teaching Practice Assessment by a super-
visor. The subjectivity of this approach, and its inconsistency as a
guide to long term effectiveness and success as a teacher, is legendary
(See, for example, Robertson 1957, Stones and Morris 1972). Nonetheless, it remains a reality in many teacher training institutions, and
anything which assists trainee teachers to improve their assessments,
must be worthy of closer examination, at least as a potential adjunct
to present practices.

Pope reproduces the diagram (on the facing page), comparing the
Teaching Practice Assessments obtained by students who took part in
the study.

She notes:

It can be seen from this that the trend is for those within the
'grids with feedback' group to obtain higher Teacher Practice
Assessments than those who completed grids, and that those
who completed grids only had higher assessments than those
who were interviewed without completing grids. Given that there
was no contact between myself and the college staff as to who

volunteered to take part in the study and that the staff were
unaware of the full details of the project, these results are
encouraging.

(Pope, 1978, p 85)

```
                TEACHING PRACTICE
                   ASSESSMENT
                                          G
   %                                      R
                                          A
                                          D
           NG    G    FG                  E    NG    G    FG

                                          1

   65

                                          1/2

   60

                                          2

   55

                                          2/3

   50
```

COLLEGE 1   COLLEGE 2

KEY FG = FEEDBACK GROUP
     G = GRID ONLY GROUP
     NG = NO GRID GROUP

Teaching practice assessment obtained by subjects

(Pope, 1978, Reproduced by Permission Academic Press Inc. (London)
Ltd)

Pope's research has several interesting dimensions. For a start, by eliciting the elements which were later used as a basis for the repertory grids, an interesting insight was obtained into the issues which concern trainee teachers. Pope says, for instance,

> On obtaining the list of elements at the outset, I was immediately struck by the fact that, despite many conversations with student teachers before this study, I would not have provided needing adult company as an element. This, however, proved to be a very important element as far as this particular student teacher was concerned. It was one of the reasons behind her decision to enter teacher training.
>
> (Pope, 1978, p 79)

A second dimension, and indeed the crux of Pope's research, concerned the value, to individual student teachers, of gaining some insight into their individual patterns of construing. It appears that not only did trainee teachers value the opportunity to reflect on their personal approach to teaching, but that such self awareness may have enhanced their respective teaching practice assessments.

Thirdly, Pope's results corroborate a great deal of other research which emphasizes the importance of teaching practice to the student teacher (see, for example, Clark and Nisbet in Wragg, 1974). It is in this latter area, that two other researchers, Adams-Webber and Mirc, have used the repertory grid procedures "to assess the development of student teachers' conceptions of their future professional roles during the first six weeks of practice teaching experience" (Adams-Webber, 1979, p 190).

A brief outline of the research is as follows:-

> The basic assumption of this research was that individual teachers evolve specific subsystems of interrelated constructs in terms of which they define their own pattern of involvement in routine activities such as instruction, testing, and counselling, etc. Their role subsystems can be viewed as also having implications for how the various functions of the teacher role are coordinated with those of related roles (e.g. pupil, principal, school librarian) within the school system. It was hypothesized that there would be gradual increases in the level of integration of student teachers' role subsystems as they gained classroom experience. Also, Kelly's (1955) assumption that there is a high

degree of specialisation among subsystems within an individual's personal construct system implies that these changes should be specific to their teacher role subsystems and not generalize to other sectors of their construct systems.

The principals of seven schools – randomly selected from all primary schools in the same Canadian city (pop. 120, 000) – individually completed the following repertory grid task. Each principal was shown a list of ten 'role titles' (e. g. teacher, principal, pupil etc.) and asked to nominate one individual who occupied each of these positions in his own school... and he was asked to indicate which figure was most involved in, say, "handling discipline problems". This procedure was repeated until he had rank-ordered all ten figures from most to least involved in this function. Next, he ranked the same figures in terms of their degree of involvement in a second function, say pupil promotion – and so on – until he had successively ranked them on the basis of their degree of participation in the nineteen different functions (constructs) listed in the Table.

Activity Constructs

---

1. Defining teaching objectives
2. Designing tests
3. Marking tests
4. Handling discipline problems
5. Pupil promotion
6. Budget spending
7. Referral to other staff
8. Writing reports on pupils
9. Organization of timetable
10. Assessing effectiveness of learning programme
11. Assessing effectiveness of teachers
12. Controlling use of learning materials
13. Determining teachers' workloads
14. Determining what is to be learned
15. Participation in classroom learning
16. Participation in out-of-school learning
17. Deciding where learning occurs
18. Determining emphasis on reading, writing, maths, etc.
19. Determining emphasis on dance, singing, art, etc.

(From Adams-Webber, 1979, p 191)

The data elicited from each principal were arranged in a separate ten-column (roles) by nineteen-row (constructs) matrix. These data indicate a fairly high level of interjudge agreement considering that each principal rank-ordered a different set of individuals. This suggests that they shared similar conceptions of the function of each role within their schools.

Next, sixty-four regular classroom teachers, recruited from the same schools, individually completed the same repertory grid task. A single coefficient of concordance was computed independently for each teacher's grid. A single integration score was also computed for each principal. A positive correlation was found between the integration score of each principal and the median integration score of the teachers in his own school (Spearman $r = 0.75$; $p < .05$). This suggests a fairly high degree of interaction between the role subsystems of principals and teachers working under them.

Finally, twenty-nine student teachers, enrolled in a practice-teaching course in the College of Education, Brock University - none of whom had previous teaching experience and all of whom planned to become teachers - individually completed the same repertory grid task during the first week of the course prior to any practice teaching and on three subsequent occasions, following each of three fortnightly sessions during which they were engaged on a daily basis in supervised teaching in local schools. Each of these sessions was spent in a different school. As a control for the possible effects of repeating the same repertory grid format, an additional grid task was completed on each occasion.

These data showed, as was predicted, significant increases in the students' integration scores across the four experimental grids ($x^2 = 15.44$; 3 df; $p < .01$) and no significant changes across the four control grids ($x^2 = 1.10$; 3 df; NS). This result is consistent with the hypothesis that there would be gradual increases in the level of integration of the students' role subsystems as they acquired classroom experience. The fact that there were no systematic changes in the control grids rules out the possibility that the increases observed in the experimental grids were due to the mere repetition of the same grid format; and it also lends support to the second hypothesis that the expected increases in integration would be specific to those constructs which are directly relevant to structuring the teacher role and would not generalize to other sectors of their personal construct systems.

Comparisons between the students' grids and those of the regular classroom teachers indicated that before engaging in any practice teaching the students' integration scores were significantly lower than those of the teachers ($z = -2.97$; $p < .01$); however, after only six weeks in the classroom they had developed role subsystems which did not differ in terms of their overall level of integration from those of experienced teachers.

(Adams-Webber, 1979, pp 190-192)

It is important to note that this research, although using the repertory grid technique, was carried out within an essentially nomothetic framework, where individual differences in construing have been evened out to give an overall impression. It may well be that some student teachers did not significantly alter their construct systems in the direction of the publicly agreed role functions, but the research findings do tend to support the notion of more highly integrated construct subsystems as a result of certain types of professional experience.

This apparent tendency for the construct systems of student teachers to begin to resemble those of more experienced colleagues, brings me to a consideration of the use of Kelly's Repertory Grid in the Staff Development of teachers in-service. Keen sees Repertory Grids as a way of drawing certain tacit assumptions made by a teacher to his/her attention. Keen's approach requires the subject to complete a single grid, using elements supplied, which is then subjected to intensive analysis. The results of this analysis, which are presented in the form of several profiles or graphs, are returned to the respondent, who is invited to contemplate them, and if desired, to discuss them with the project directors. The ultimate intention is to provide, for the respondent, an individualised development programme.

Keen has devised an ingenious way of providing elements for each subject to use in eliciting a grid. The elements comprise the name of the person undertaking the exercise ('self'), the names of the most effective and most ineffective teachers known to the subject, and then eleven other teachers, with widely varying styles, of whom the subject is shown videotaped excerpts:

The videotape is carefully constructed in order to representatively sample the construct space of the respondent, a test being incorporated into the analysis which ensures that, for any individual respondent, his cognitive structure has indeed been representatively and adequately explored by the videotaped excerpts.

(Hopwood and Keen, 1978, p 190)

Keen does not specify exactly how he manages to ensure that he <u>has</u> 'sampled the construct space of the respondent', and indeed it is difficult to imagine how he could do so, considering the complex and unique nature of each person's construct system. Interestingly, another researcher writes of Keen's technique:

Having responded to such a grid I found myself using superficial discriminations between the videotaped elements because they were unfamiliar teachers, the majority of whom were using a lecturing approach in a microteaching format: other constructs which might have been elicited were not encouraged to emerge.

(Yorke, 1978, p 64)

The grid is completed, up to about twenty construct pairs, using a five point rating scale to rate all the elements (names of teachers) on each set of constructs. Triads are selected on the basis of a pilot study in order to facilitate the elicitation of independent constructs. The grid thus completed is analysed by means of a computer programme called TARGET, which is an acronym for Teaching Appraisal by Repertory Grid Elicitation Technique.

This programme, which is an extension of Slater's Grid Analysis Package, identifies principal components made up of elements and constructs, and indicates how many such Principal Components seem to be operating for each respondent. The results are printed out in the form of bar charts,

designed to give an immediate visual impression of the characteristics present or absent in the pedagogic style represented by that profile. There will be a number of bars either to the left or to the right of the central vertical line. The number of bars found to be significant in the analysis is clearly indicated. A respondent with more than four significant bars (some respondents have up to 11) has an ability to appraise a teaching act, be it personal or otherwise, in an open and unbiassed manner. However, less

than three significant bars on his profile indicates a distinctly
lower-than-average ability to recognise and appreciate differing
pedagogic practices for their intrinsic worth.

(Hopwood and Keen, 1978, p 192)

Whilst it is an intuitively appealing notion that more bars mean a better
balanced approach to teaching, it must be noted that there is considerable controversy surrounding the reliability of Slater's Grid Analysis
Package, and furthermore, bearing in mind Yorke's comment above,
that trivial constructs may be elicited ahead of significant ones, some
doubt must attach to the statistical precision which Keen seems to
claim. I will discuss this point in more detail later, but many researchers maintain that a major part of the value in completing a grid, lies in
discussing it with others, rather than merely subjecting it to computer
analysis and waiting for trends and patterns to emerge. Indeed, Keen
seems implicitly to acknowledge this himself, when he discusses the
importance of counselling respondents.

Each person undertaking the experience is given three of the computer
profiles, showing respectively:

   (a) his/her perception of an effective teaching style
   (b) his/her perception of own teaching style
   (c) his/her perception of an ineffective teaching style.

It is almost inevitable that a teacher, on receiving his profiles,
will immediately compare one with another. On comparing his
own teaching style profile with that perceived by him to be
representative of effective teaching, he may conclude that there
is some inadequacy or deficiency in his own teaching style. It is
at this point that the need arises for the provision of a consult-
ancy or counselling service...

(Hopwood and Keen, 1978, p 189)

In discussing the usefulness of this approach, Keen readily admits that
quantifiable data are hard to obtain; his faith in the usefulness of the
approach being largely based on positive feedback from users. Concerning the statistical reliability of the method, he admits that test-retest
reliability is poor, but attributes this to the fact that 'exposure to the
feedback does alter the respondent's perception, both of himself and of
effective teaching', which corroborates Pope's finding about the differences obtained by respondents, with and without feedback.

Yorke, in an article concerning Repertory Grids in Educational Research, rightly points out the difficulty of providing elements which are 'a valid and representative sample of the field under study'. He goes on:

> ... if one wishes to study perceptions of <u>teaching</u>, the elements should be teaching <u>situations</u> rather than teachers themselves. To select the latter, which are mediations of teaching, would tend to emphasise teaching style or teachers' characteristics (Perrott et al, 1976; Hopwood and Keen, 1978) at the expense of a more penetrating analysis of the way in which the respondent construes teaching itself.
>
> (Yorke, 1978, p 64)

Consequently, Yorke's elements comprise brief descriptions of teaching situations, which are used to elicit constructs; each situation is stated in a phrase but elaborated in a sentence on a separate sheet in an attempt to ensure a common language framework between researcher and interviewees, and amongst the respondents themselves. One particularly innovative component of Yorke's methodology is his use of a modified form of Hinkle's "Resistance to Change" Grid. Since the elements are situations and not people, there is not the possibility to include 'self' as an element. Therefore, in order to make the exercise more personally relevant and immediate, he asks each respondent to indicate which end of each construct pair is most like themselves. These 'preferred poles' can then be presented two at a time to the subject, who is asked on which one they would rather change to the opposite pole (unless a change in one automatically necessitated a change in the other, or a change in either would be equally undesirable). The result is a league table, showing from the most to the least, the flexibility of the subject on each of his/her own constructs. (See Bannister and Fransella, 1977, p 45.)

CONCLUSION

In this Chapter, I have briefly reviewed several examples of the use of Repertory Grid Technique in the field of Teacher Training. I have demonstrated its use in two, essentially different ways. In the first, the Technique is used as a teaching instrument and, as Thomas and Harri-Augstein state, "the process of conversationally eliciting a grid is in itself a learning experience, both for the elicitor and subject. When successful, it raises awareness of the underlying processes

whereby thoughts and feelings combine to give meaning to events".
(Thomas and Harri-Augstein, 1977, p 91).

In the case of the Adams-Webber and Mirc research, however, the
technique was used nomothetically. Whilst the results are instrinsically
interesting, (and we can reasonably assume that respondents also
learned something from the experience) it is worth remembering that
such use of the grid confronts the same sort of problems as any other
research project or experiment.

> Although it is an often repeated truism that the grid method is
> not a test, it is still a largely ignored truism.

> This is exemplified in our constant failure to recognise that the
> use of a grid involves all the kinds of problems that we confront
> in designing an experiment. Whatever the question being
> experimentally asked, to use a grid is to involve the researcher
> in a whole series of problems. These concern the nature of the
> elements to be used, forms of construct elicitation and the
> format (e.g. ranking, rating or bi-polar allotment) in which the
> subject is to respond. Additionally there are a multiplicity of
> ways in which grid data can be analysed and many kinds of in-
> ference it is legitmate to draw from them. Yet whether the focus
> of concern is with an individual case... or large scale research,
> grids tend to be too readily used and the user is often buried in
> the mountains of data which are generated.
> (Fransella and Bannister, 1977, p 9)

But worse by far than this vision of the investigator slowly disappearing
under a tide of information, is the spectre of Kelly's noble image of
"Man the scientist", unceremoniously interred in some bizarre reversal
of grave robbing. Once again, the old paradigm insidiously re-emerging,
of the respondent generating data for the researcher, with his own learning needs ignored. In 1969, Kelly even suggested that the subject should
be involved in the process of designing the research approach - surely
it is not too much to expect the researcher to honour the spirit of
Kelly's theory, at least in going back to the respondent for analysis and
clarification of the data? After all, whose grid is it anyway?

CHAPTER V

PERSONAL CONSTRUCTS IN ADULT EDUCATION

In this last chapter, I would like to venture a few speculative comments about how Kelly's Theory of Personal Constructs can be linked into certain central concerns of adult education. At first sight, this may appear tangential to the main thrust of this monograph (which is the training of teachers of adults), but a moment's reflection should show otherwise.

The training of teachers should, but often does not, conform to adult learning principles. Brundage and MacKeracher write:

> (There is a) contradiction between basic child and adult learning goals and processes. For children, learning focusses largely on socializing and conforming to group norms and on forming meanings, values, skills and strategies. The teacher-learner must acquire the processes and strategies necessary to promote these types of learning. As an adult, the teacher-learner is focussing largely on solving personal problems, acquiring necessary role behaviours, and transforming meanings, values, skills and strategies. He will learn through the processes most relevant to adult learning. To the extent that child-related processes and adult-related processes are different, the teacher-learner may experience some confusion. This confusion is often compounded by learning programs for teachers designed on the basis of child-related learning processes.
> (Brundage and MacKeracher, 1980, p 88)

Although this assertion itself may be contentious, my point in raising this issue is not to open the question of differences between adults and children as learners, nor indeed to pass judgement on the training of child educators, but rather to focus on the similarities between adults and adult educators, as learners. Elsdon, writing about Training for Adult Education, states:

> The clearest message implicit in any view of training for adult education in England today is that it has become adult education

for adult educators. It has its special applications to their function as such, but it is perceived, felt and enthusiastically engaged in like ordinary adult education raised, as it were, to a higher power. Adult educators are adults after all. The principles on which their training is founded must therefore be considered in the same terms as those of adult education in general....

(Elsdon, 1975, p 57)

And Campbell echoes this sentiment:

The form and purpose of training adult educators ought certainly to be at least as effective as the form and purpose employed in the provision of adult education to adults generally. Training for adult education ought to demonstrate, indeed to epitomize, the principles inherent in adult education.

(Campbell, 1977, p 89)

This principle of reflexivity is very important. A body which teaches others how to manage, has a duty of care to be well managed; an institution which trains social workers will usually attempt to abide by the principles of self-determination, personal reponsibility and unconditional personal regard which it espouses. Universities, Colleges and other places of teacher training should, if their practice is not to belie their principles, strive for excellence in teaching, and this is absolutely true, the sine qua non, of training adult educators - the practice must be congruent with the theory.

This is more than a mere preoccupation with neatness and consistency, the evidence on the impact of modelling as a way of teaching is too well known to need repeating here, (see, for example, Bandura, 1977). The simple fact is that student teachers will typically absorb infinitely more from the unspoken attitudes and modes of behaviour of their mentors, than from all the lectures on educational theory put together.

What, then, are the central principles of adult education, to which the training of adult educators should pay attention? There are many suggestions in the literature, however, there is little agreement as to which of these features constitute the central concerns or identifying characteristics of the field of adult education. For the purpose of this chapter, therefore, I have selected the following four notions which, for me, have a central place in the enterprise of educating adults.

- The Philosophy of Lifelong Learning
- The Principle of Self-Direction
- The Central Importance of Experience
- The Concept and Importance of Individual Differences

It is recognised that these four areas are neither exhaustive, nor mutually exclusive and indeed, as the following examination of Kelly's Theory shows, there is a high degree of interdependence between these characteristics of adult learning.

LIFELONG EDUCATION AND LIFELONG LEARNING

Lifelong Education

The educational lexicon has, in recent years, been enriched by the phrase 'lifelong education'. Numerous books and articles have been written about it (see, for example, Jessup 1969, Lengrand 1970, Dave 1973 and 1976, Parkyn 1973, Duke 1976, Cropley 1977), and it has been proposed by the International Commission on the Development of Education (Faure 1972) "as the master concept for educational policies in the years to come for both developed and developing countries". It may be defined as follows.

> (Lifelong education) is a very comprehensive idea which includes formal as well as non-formal learning extended throughout the lifespan of an individual to attain the fullest possible development in personal, social and professional life. It includes all desired learning that occurs in a planned or incidental way in the home, educational institutions, community and place of work. Lifelong education encompasses all stages and aspects of education in an integrated and articulated manner.
>
> (Dave, 1973, p 30)

There are two notions which are central to the philosophy of lifelong education. The first is

> the conviction that all individuals ought to have organised and systematic opportunities for instruction, study and learning at any time throughout their lives. This is true whether their goals are to remedy earlier educational defects, to acquire new skills, to upgrade themselves vocationally, to increase their understanding of the world in which they live, to develop their own personalities or some other purposes.
>
> (Cropley, 1977, p 21)

The second is "the belief that learning... occurs throughout life, albeit in different ways and through differing processes." (Cropley, 1977, p 21).

It is easy to lose sight of the fact that a system of lifelong education has implications for learners and potential learners of all ages, however, I am concentrating here on the education of adults. The idea of continuing educational opportunities for adults is not particularly new. Writing about informal adult education in the ancient world, Anderson states

> Perhaps the most interesting aspect of Graeco-Roman education is its system of extensive and frequently used facilities for all sorts of informal adult education... The classical institutions... embody the principles that real learning is for adulthood, and that education is a desirable thing - principles which are by no means as universally accepted in the modern world as they were by the masses of the ancient world...
>
> (Anderson, 1974, p 1)

The need for education throughout life has been a recurring theme. "Education is not an affair of childhood and youth, it is the business of the whole life", wrote J. Hole as early as 1853, and the British Ministry of Reconstruction Adult Education Report of 1919 concluded: "adult education is a permanent national necessity, an inseparable aspect of citizenship, and therefore should be both universal and lifelong...."

In his 1941 book The Future of Education, Sir Richard Livingstone argued not only that "adults should have recurring opportunities to think over their occupations in later life and to study new developments and knowledge", but also that there were certain subjects, "politics, economics, religion and the conduct of life" which we should study "after the age of thirty" because we are so much better equipped to study them then, than "as a schoolboy or undergraduate".

It seems, then, that the need for adults to have access to continuing educational opportunities has considerable historical support. With the rapid pace of social and technological change today, the need for lifelong education is, if anything, even more pressing.

It is hard to believe that the following prophetic statement was written fifty years ago

... in the past, the span of important change was considerably longer than that of a single human life. Thus mankind was trained to adapt itself to fixed conditions.

Today, this time span is considerably shorter than that of human life and accordingly our training must prepare individuals to face a novelty of conditions.

(Whitehead, 1929, p 118)

As Lengrand asserts, "the notion that a man can accomplish his lifespan with a given set of intellectual and technical luggage is fast disappearing". (Lengrand, 1970, p 44)

There is a remarkable degree of unanimity about the desirability of the concept of lifelong education, and indeed, as Dave points out, it has "recently emerged as a significant organising principle for all education". (Dave, 1973, p 29) According to Rodriguez, "the still highly abstract nature of the idea facilitates the emergence of an almost universal consensus in its favour... Only a very few discordant voices are raised to warn against the danger of totalitarianism". (Rodriguez, 1972, p 27)

Indeed, there are very few people who would object to the idea that people should have a right to education throughout life. Such objectors as Illich and Ohliger argue not so much against the need for lifelong educational opportunities, as against the excessive formalisation of the systems; against the "technocrats, politicians and educationists of a commercial and efficient society (who) gang up together to expand schooling to a lifetime in order to equip people better for the demands of the economy and thus the demands of productivity".

Lifelong Learning

Important as this debate is, it is not my intention to pursue the question of lifelong education here. Instead, I wish to focus on the major pillar which supports it, namely, the concept of lifelong learning. Although the terms 'lifelong education' and 'lifelong learning' are often used interchangeably, I am arguing here that they do not mean the same thing:

> Learning and education are not synonymous. Education is a term that implies the provision of conditions that will facilitate learning. Lifelong learning and lifelong education, then, are not identical concepts.

(Parkyn, 1973, p 9)

What support is there for a notion of lifelong learning? Thomas More (in his Utopia), Comenius and Condorcet all stressed that learning throughout life should be basic to human development, and likewise both Chinese and Hindu philosophy have insisted for thousands of years that learning should continue from "womb to tomb" (and indeed, even beyond, to other lives as well). Under the heading "New Significance of an Old Idea", Dave writes

> If one fathoms the ancient literature of different civilisations, one soon discovers that the idea of lifelong learning is indeed a very old one. And one could argue that lifelong learning was always going on in one form or another without it developing into an educational principle and often without it being a conscious act. This is because learning is natural for human beings at any stage in life, and there is always a need to learn something new as long as one is active and alive.
>
> The need to continue learning throughout life stems from various forces. For example, one of the mainsprings of lifelong learning is the change in social roles that every individual is confronted with right from infancy to old age. Another mainspring of lifelong learning is the physiological growth and change occurring at different stages of life. There are several other factors - social, economic, cultural and those pertaining to the inner, personal life - that necessitate acquisition of new skills, knowledge and attitudes, and relearning or even unlearning of what was acquired before. These forces have been operating from time immemorial, and they continue to operate perennially, influencing all human beings in developed as well as developing countries.
>
> (Dave, 1973, p 11)

It seems strange, in the face of statements like this one, that people such as William James could assert that anyone over the age of 25 has great difficulty in carrying out new learning. And it is not simply that James was writing in 1890, for similar views are still widely (though often tacitly) held, even today.

The controversy surrounding adult learning highlights a very important (though often ignored) distinction, namely that between formal or intentional learning, and informal or incidental learning. The prevailing sterotype about adults' inability to learn has been predominantly in the sphere of intentional learning. Interestingly, there is now accumulating a vast bank of research findings to question, and in many cases overturn, the conventional wisdom that adults cannot learn, though to be sure, there <u>are</u> differences both amongst adult learners and between more mature and younger learners. On balance it seems to me beyond question that "almost any adult is able to learn almost any subject given sufficient time and attention" (Knox, 1977, p 464), and there is certainly a well established psychological basis to support a system of lifelong education. The notion that adults can learn informally (i. e. unintentionally or incidentally in the course of doing something else) also seems well established.

Few if any people would disagree with Knox when he writes, "Adults continually learn informally as they adjust to role changes and in various ways achieve adaptation and growth" (Knox, 1977, p 463) or Cropley; "adults clearly achieve enormous amounts of social learning, to an extent that makes it clear that they can, and habitually do, adapt and adjust to their environments (i. e. learn)." (Cropley, 1977, p 74).

One particularly cogent and, in my opinion, unsurpassed statement about the linkages between learning and living, was made by Dewey in the early years of this century. Parkyn summarises Dewey's proposition in the following terms:

> Life, stated Dewey, is a process of development, and developing is living. This process is not simply a spontaneous unfolding of latent potentialities, little affected by the environment, nor is it simply a forming or shaping by external stimuli. At all stages it is a transaction between a living being and its surroundings, a transaction in which the living being mentally or physically transforms or reconstructs those parts of its environment that are relevant to its life. In so doing it transforms itself and enhances the quality of its life. The value of the process of transformation lies in its continued enhancement of the quality of living. Development leads to the possibility of further development.

> Human beings are essentially social beings, and the environmental conditions within which they develop are in the main socially created. They include all aspects of man's culture, his knowledge, skills, attitudes, customs, laws, beliefs, values, and so on. Their transformation takes place not by mere physical ingestion and digestion as in the intake of food, but by perceiving, conceiving, enlarging the range of meaning of experience, by learning. The value of learning lies in the extent to

which it enriches experience. It is, indeed, says Dewey, "the chief business of life at every point to make living thus contribute to an enhancement of its own perceptible meaning." (Dewey, 1916, p 90).

(Parkyn, 1973, p 9)

Kelly and Lifelong Learning

In his original book, the Psychology of Personal Constructs, Kelly writes,

> For example, the term learning so honourably embedded in most psychological texts, scarcely appears at all. This is wholly intentional; for we are throwing it overboard altogether.
>
> (Kelly, 1955, p x)

And, to make doubly certain, in a paper posthumously published in 1977, Kelly again states:

> I even once found it (personal construct psychology) categorised as a 'learning' theory, a discovery which has given me considerable amusement since, in proposing the theory, I went to some lengths to urge psychologists to consider the advantages of abandoning the concept of 'learning' altogether.
>
> (Kelly, 1977, p 13)

In the light of the foregoing, it is difficult to see, at least at first glance, what possible support and comfort Kelly's theory might offer for a concept of lifelong learning. In fact, it is necessary to find out why Kelly eschews learning and what he suggests in its place. In dispensing with the notion of 'learning' per se, Kelly writes:

> The burden of our assumption is that learning is not a special class of psychological processes; it is synonymous with any and all psychological processes. It is not something that happens to a person on occasion; it is what makes him a person in the first place.
>
> (Kelly, 1955, p 75)

This then raises the question, what sort of people does Kelly think we are? And here, of course, we encounter his notion of 'man-the-scientist'. In several places, Kelly explains the idea:

> When we speak of man-the-scientist, we are speaking of all mankind, and not merely a particular class of men who have

publicly attained the stature of 'scientists'.... What is it that is supposed to characterize the motivation of the scientist? It is customary to say that the scientist's ultimate aim is to predict and control. This is a summary statement that psychologists frequently like to quote in characterizing their own aspirations. Yet, curiously enough, psychologists rately credit the human subjects in their experiments with having similar aspirations.... Might not the individual man, each in his own personal way, assume more of the stature of a scientist, ever seeking to predict and control the course of events with which he is involved? Would he not have his theories, test his hypotheses, and weigh his experimental evidence?

(Kelly, 1955, p 4-5)

We now have a picture of people prepared to test out their hypotheses about life, and to attempt to make sense of their experiences in a systematic way. What, then, is the mechanism whereby life experience is converted into what we might conventionally call lifelong learning?

Kelly begins by explaining that events never repeat themselves exactly - there are always differences which allow for individual experiences to be distinguished. It is the purpose of our construct systems, to simultaneously identify similarities and differences - for "under a system that provides only for the identification of similarities, the world dissolves into homogeneity, under one that provides only for differentiation, it is shattered into hopelessly unrelated fragments." (Kelly, 1970, p 11). He goes on:

> Keeping in mind that events do not repeat themselves and that the replication we talk about is a replication of ascribed aspects only, it begins to be clear that the succession we call experience is based on the constructions we place on what goes on. If those constructions are never altered, all that happens during a man's years is a sequence of parallel events having no psychological impact on his life. But if he invests himself... in the enterprise, the outcome to the extent that it differs from his expectation or enlarges upon it, dislodges the man's construction of himself... confirmation may lead to reconstruing as much as disconfirmation.

(Kelly, 1970, p 18)

As has already been stated, this process of construing and reconstruing is as Kelly says "not something that happens to a person on occasion, it

is what makes him a person in the first place". Kelly consistently
emphasizes that the process of construing is a lifelong and perpetual
one - "each man contemplates in his own way the stream of events
upon which he finds himself so swiftly borne." (Kelly, 1955, p 3).

It appears, then, that if we explore what lies at the heart of Kelly's
Theory, we discover that it is nothing, if not a psychology of lifelong
learning. Or, to put it another way, if we dispense with the words
'lifelong learning' and substitute Dewey's dictum that "the chief business of life at every point (is) to make living contribute to an enhancement of its own percpetible meaning", we find that this is precisely
what Kelly is saying, only in slightly different terms:

> If it were a static world that we lived in, our thinking about it
> might be static too. But new things keep happening and our
> predictions keep turning out in expected or unexpected ways.
> Each day's experience calls for the consolidation of some aspects
> of our outlook, revision of some, outright abandonment of others.
>
> (Kelly, 1955, p 14)

THE PRINCIPLE OF SELF-DIRECTION

> Originally, all human knowledge was nothing more than the
> knowledge of a comparatively small number of such facts as
> those from which Galileo deduced the use of the pendulum for
> the measurement of time, and Newton the explanation of the sys-
> tem of the heavens. All the rest of our knowledge, and these
> first rudiments of it also, a succession of individuals have
> gradually discovered, each by his own portion, by their own
> efforts and without having any teacher to instruct them. In other
> words, everything that is actually known has been found out and
> learned by some person or other, without the aid of an instruc-
> tor. There is no species of learning, therefore, which even self-
> education may not overtake; for there is none which it has not
> actually overtaken. All discoverers... have been self-taught
> at least in regard to that which they have discovered.
>
> (Craik, 1866, p 13)

If there is any one feature which is consistently held up as the identifying
characteristic of adult education, it is the ability, and indeed the propen-
sity, of adult learners to be self-directed; to "take the initiative, with
or without the help of others in diagnosing their learning needs,

formulating learning goals, identifying human and material resources for learning, choosing and implementing appropriate learning strategies, and evaluating learning outcomes". (Knowles, 1975, p 18).

Probably the most exhaustive survey of self-direction in adult learning is Tough's The Adult's Learning Projects a monograph in which he explores the phenomenon of self-directed learning projects. He reports:

> Almost everyone undertakes at least one or two major learning efforts a year, and some individuals undertake as many as 15 or 20. The median is eight learning projects a year, involving eight distinct areas of knowledge and skill.

> A learning project is simply a major, highly deliberate effort to gain certain knowledge and skill (or to change in some other way). Some learning projects are efforts to gain new knowledge, insight, or understanding. Others are attempts to improve one's skill or performance, or to change one's attitudes or emotional reactions. Others involve efforts to change one's overt behaviour or to break a habit.

> It is common for a man or woman to spend 700 hours a year at learning projects. Some persons spend less than 100 hours, but others spend more than 2000 hours in episodes in which the person's intent to learn or change is clearly his primary motivation.

> Many learning projects are initiated for highly practical reasons: to make a good decision, build something, or carry out some task related to one's job, home, family, sport, or hobby. Adult learning is also motivated by curiosity, interest, and enjoyment. A few projects are motivated by credit toward a degree or certificate.
> (Tough, 1971, p 1)

However, self-direction should not be confused with independent study - it describes the degree of learner control, rather than the independence of study method. The realisation that adults are, above all self-directed learners, has been steadily gaining ground in recent years. There has been a steadily expanding stream of literature devoted to exploring the phenomenon and, in many cases, its corollary which is the decline in the transmittal role of the teacher. Terms like guide, mentor, learning manager, resource person and facilitator, have progressively replaced the more strictly didactic word 'teacher', but this is more than mere semantic sleight of hand - it represents a significant shift in the balance of control. The Faure Report comments:

> From the standpoint of lifelong education, and in the present state of human knowledge, calling teachers 'masters' (whichever of its meanings we give the word) is more and more an abuse of the term. The teacher's duty is less and less to inculcate knowledge, and more and more to encourage thinking; his formal functions apart, he will have to become increasingly an adviser, a partner to talk to, someone who seeks out conflicting arguments rather than handing out ready-made truths. He will have to devote more time and energy to productive and creative activities, interaction, discussion, stimulation, understanding, encouragement.
>
> (Faure, 1972, pp 77/8)

The notion that adults are self-directing is, conceptually at least, a very powerful one. Knowles, the adult educator whose name is most closely linked with the idea of self-directed learning, has progressively refined both his andragogical methodology, and its supporting statement of philosophy. In discussing the assumptions underlying Teacher-Directed and Self-Directed Learning, he writes:

> (One) assumption is that as a <u>person grows and matures his self-concept moves from one of total dependency</u> (as is the reality of the infant) <u>to one of increasing self-directedness</u>. It is my observation that in our culture an individual's need and capacity to be self-directing develop much faster than our institutions (especially the home, the church, and the school) provide for, and that by adolescence the gap between self-perception and cultural perception of self-directedness reaches its apogee - and that this is what the student rebellion is all about.

> Andragogy assumes that the point at which an individual achieves a self-concept of essential self-direction is the point at which he psychologically becomes adult. A very critical thing happens when this occurs; the individual develops a deep psychological need to be perceived by others as being self-directing. Thus, <u>when he finds himself in a situation in which he is not allowed to be self-directing, he experiences a tension between that situation and his self-concept</u>. His reaction is bound to be tainted with resentment and resistance.
>
> (Knowles, 1972)

Kelly's concept of <u>man-the-scientist</u> is very congruent with Knowles'
view of <u>man-the-self-directed learner</u> - both strongly reject the
behaviourist paradigm. Kelly dispenses with the <u>push</u> theories based on
stimuli, and the <u>pull</u> theories based on needs, and states:

> Instead of buying the prior assumption of an inert object, either
> on an implicit or explicit basis, we propose to postulate a pro-
> cess as the point of departure for the formulation of a psycho-
> logical theory. Thus, the whole controversy as to what prods an
> inert organism into action becomes a dead issue. Instead, the
> organism is delivered fresh into the psychological world, alive
> and struggling.
>
> (Kelly, 1955, p 37)

This seems quite a promising beginning for someone to be self-directed.
Kelly goes on:

> Like the prototype of the scientist that he is, man seeks predic-
> tion. His structured network of pathways leads towards the
> future so that he may anticipate it. This is the function it serves.
> Anticipation is both the push and pull of the psychology of per-
> sonal constructs.
>
> (Kelly, 1955, p 49)

It seems then, that Kelly postulates that we are indeed self-directing.
Not occasionally, but perpetually - by our very nature, people are in
perpetual motion, seeking to predict and to understand their worlds.
Though, as I have already pointed out, Kelly is at great pains to do
away with the concept of learning by equating it with "any and all
psychological processes", it is hard to escape the conclusion that he
would endorse the characterisation of people as 'self-directed learners'.

INDIVIDUAL DIFFERENCES AND THE ROLE OF EXPERIENCE

The question of whether individual learners differ from one another in
significant ways has received a great deal of scholarly attention,
expecially recently. This is true of learners in all age groups - adults
and children alike.

Likewise, the interaction between inherent characteristics or predispositions, and one's life experiences (often summed up as the nature-
nurture debate) is another massive and seemingly intractable area of
contention.

This section starts off from the naively simple, yet hopefully widely accepted position that learners do differ from one another in ways which influence their learning, and that these differences are, at least partly, due to experience (both educational and otherwise). It is hoped to show that Kelly's Personal Construct Theory sheds some light on these issues, in respect of the education of adults.

Individual Differences

Psychologists generally, and educational psychologists in particular, have long been perplexed by the apparent contradiction inherent in the proposition that all people are alike, yet all people are different. Of course, both assertions are true in part, and it is probably fair to say that many debates in education revolve around which statement is 'truer' for any particular situation. Certainly, the recent trend towards individualisation in instruction, rests on the assumption that, for the purposes of teaching and learning, individual differences are more important than similarities. Cross writes:

> it now seems clear that we are not going to improve instruction by finding the method or methods that are good for all people. The research on teaching effectiveness has been inconclusive and disappointing because I suspect, we were asking the wrong questions. When we ask whether discussion is better than lecture, whether television is as good as a live teacher, whether programmed instruction is an improvement over traditional methods, we find that for the mythical statistical average student it seems to make little difference how we teach. But when we look at the data student by student, it is clear that some students improve, some remain unaffected, and a few actually regress under various teaching conditions. The very process of averaging the pluses, the minuses, and the nonchangers wipes out the message that different methods work for different students. Psychologists are now asking the more sophisticated interaction questions about learning styles - which methods work for which students?
>
> (Cross, 1976, p 111)

A similar point is made by Hudson in the following terms:

> There is, after all, little merit (and no point) in proposing general ideas about human beings if these are largely or completely mistaken. Nor is there any virtue in claiming that an idea is 'basically right' although obscured by the welter of

people's individuality. It is the welter that we must observe and measure....

(Hudson, 1967, p 17)

The focus of Kelly's Theory is unequivocally idiographic. Certainly, his Sociality Corollary and Commonality Corollary "emphasise that it is in the sharing and understanding of the system used for comparing and contrasting phenomena, that similarity and understanding are rooted" (Ryle, 1975, p 12), but Kelly's statement that "Persons differ from each other in their construction of events" (individuality corollary) is, in many respects, the central theme of his Psychology of Personal Constructs.

The educational implications of such an intensely personalistic theory are manifold. The problem for someone in the role of teacher, or facilitator of learning, is probably encapsulated in the following quote from Bannister and Fransella:

It could be argued that the fundamental mystery of human psychology is covered by the question "Why is it that two people in exactly the same situation behave in different ways?" The answer is of course that they are not in the 'same' situation. Each of us sees our situation through the 'goggles' of our personal construct system. We differ from others in how we perceive and interpret a situation, what we consider important about it, what we consider its implications, the degree to which it is clear or obscure, threatening or promising, sought after or forced upon us. The situation of the two people who are behaving differently is only 'the same' from the point of view of a third person looking at it through his particular personal construct goggles.

(Bannister and Fransella, 1971, p 22)

How many of us, as teachers, have thought we were giving the same information to everyone, only to find a tremendous diversity in the understandings which our learners had gleaned from the presentation? Here, we see tangible evidence of the existence, and crucial importance of personal constructs.

The question would seem to be, where do these personal constructs come from, and how are they changed? In particular, if a group of people share some learning 'experience', does this get around the possibility of people construing verbal or written presentations differently? According to Kelly,

> Neither our constructs nor our construing systems come to us from nature, except, of course, from our own nature... We cannot say that constructs are essences distilled by the mind out of available reality. They are imposed upon events, not abstracted from them. There is only one place they come from; that is from the person who is to use them.
>
> (Kelly, 1970, p 13)

This might explain where our constructs come from initially, but Kelly and others are at great pains to point out that there is nothing fixed or immutable about our construct systems - they are constantly being refined and modified by encounters with the outside world. Bannister and Fransella explain it in these terms:

> A personal construct system is not a collection of treasured and guarded hallucinations, it is the person's guide to living. It is the repository of what he has learned, a statement of his intents, the values whereby he lives and the banner under which he fights. A personal construct system is a theory being put to perpetual test...
>
> The constructions one places upon events are working hypotheses which are about to be put to the test of experience. As our anticipations are hypotheses to be successively revised in the light of the unfolding sequence of events, a construction system undergoes a progressive evolution. The constant revision of personal construct systems is a function of incoming varying validational experience.
>
> (Bannister and Fransella, 1971, p 27)

Another way of putting this is to say that we do 'learn' from experience. The intriguing point is, however, that we are unlikely to 'learn' the same things from any given experience because, as has already been pointed out, experience is not an objective event. People perceive different things in an experience, they therefore "are likely to place rather different interpretations on the same events, and to set up rather different constructions to subsume the different sets of events which impinge on them." (Bannister and Mair, 1968, p 15).

In terms of adult learning, recent studies (e.g. Knox, 1977) have shown that adult learners differ from one another, and that these differences increase with age (for which we might substitute 'experience'). It seems to me that Knowles, when writing about the assumptions which underlie his concept of andragogy, is focussing on this important dimension:

> This assumption is that as an individual matures he accumulates an expanding reservoir of experience that causes him to become an increasingly rich resource for learning, and at the same time provides him with a broadening base to which to relate new learnings. Accordingly, in the technology of andragogy there is decreasing emphasis on the transmittal techniques of traditional teaching and increasing emphasis on experiential techniques which tap the experience of the learners and involve them in analyzing their experience. The use of lectures, canned audio-visual presentations, and assigned reading tend to fade in favor of discussion, laboratory, simulation, field experience, team project, and other action-learning techniques.
>
> There is another, more subtle reason for emphasizing the utilization of the experience of the learners. A young child identifies himself largely in terms of external definers - who his parents, brothers, and sisters are, where he lives, and to what school and church he goes. As he matures, he increasingly defines who he is by his experience. To a child experience is something that happens to him; to an adult, his experience is who he is. So in any situation in which an adult's experience is being devalued or ignored, the adult perceives this as not rejecting just his experience, but rejecting him as a person.
>
> (Knowles, 1972)

The argument to date may be summarised as follows. Individual differences are extremely important, expecially in teaching and learning. These differences are no less important, and perhaps even more so, in dealing with adults. People construe the world differently, but their construct systems are subject to continual modification from their experiences of life.

Indeed, one way to facilitate changes in construing, therefore, is to provide certain experiences, though there can be absolutely no guarantee that particular experiences will result in particular changes in construing (learning outcomes).

Learning from Experience

Nevertheless, it is probably useful to explore how and why people learn from experience, in the hope that Kelly's theory might throw some light on the enterprise of adult education. We begin with a consideration of the 'conventional wisdom' about experiential learning.

> ...all the techniques subsumed under the heading (Experiential Learning) have two features in common:-
>
> (i) they lead to meaningful learning; and
> (ii) this learning is achieved by the learner sorting things out for himself - i.e. he restructures his perceptual experiences and hence gains insight, or learning.
>
> (Boydell, 1976, p 17)

One of the authors who has put forward a model of the experiential learning cycle is Kolb. He writes:

> By combining the characteristics of learning and problem solving and conceiving of them as a single process, we can come closer to understanding how it is that man generates from his experience concepts, rules, and principles to guide his behaviour in new situations, and how he modifies these concepts in order to improve their effectiveness. This process is both active and passive, concrete and abstract. It can be conceived of as a four-stage cycle:
>
> (1) concrete experience is followed by
> (2) observation and reflection which leads to
> (3) the formation of abstract concepts and generalizations which lead to
> (4) hypotheses to be tested in future action which in turn leads to new experiences.

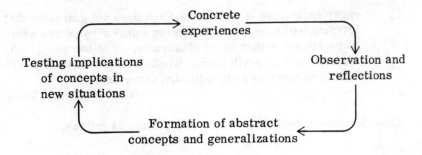

There are several observations to be made about this model of the learning process. First, this learning cycle is continuously recurring in living human beings. Man continuously tests his concepts in experience and modifies them as a result of his observation of the experience. In a very important sense, all learning is relearning and all education is re-education.

Second, the direction that learning takes is governed by one's felt needs and goals. We seek experiences that are related to our goals, interpret them in the light of our goals, and form concepts and test implications of these concepts that are relevant to our felt needs and goals. The implication of this fact is that the process of learning is erratic and inefficient when objectives are not clear.

Third, since the learning process is directed by individual needs and goals, learning styles become highly individual in both direction and process. For example, a mathematician may come to place great emphasis on abstract concepts, whereas a poet may value concrete experience more highly. A manager may be primarily concerned with active application of concepts, whereas a naturalist may develop his observational skills highly. Each of us in a more personal way develops a learning style that has some weak points and strong points. We may jump into experiences but fail to observe the lessons to be derived from these experiences; we may form concepts but fail to test their validity. In some areas our objectives, and needs may be clear guides to learning; in others, we wander aimlessly.

(Kolb, Rubin and McIntyre, 1971, pp 28-9)

A refinement of the experiential learning model is attempted by Boot and Boxer who argue:

experience alone is not learning and does not guarantee that learning will take place. It is no use providing people with 'experiences' either in the classroom, or in the workplace, in the hope that they will learn. Whether or not they learn will depend on what they 'do' with that experience.

(Boot and Boxer, 1979, p 1)

They introduce a modified version of the cycle as follows:

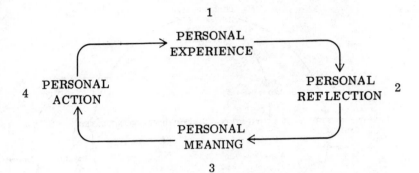

1

PERSONAL
EXPERIENCE

4 PERSONAL
ACTION

PERSONAL
REFLECTION 2

PERSONAL
MEANING

3

For us, the major aspect of learning is <u>not</u> change in overt behaviour as a result of experience, but the process of discovering new, personal meanings in that experience. Those meanings may lead to new forms of personal action and so be observable in terms of changed behaviour, but equally they may not. The stage in the cycle that influences the quality of learning from experience (i.e. the extent to which it leads to new meaning) is reflection - the process of thinking back on, reworking, or searching for meanings in experience.

(Boot and Boxer, 1979, p 2)

Based on this line of reasoning, Boot and Boxer have developed an interactive computer programme which allows people to explore their own structures of meaning.

Beck has suggested another modification which, if I understand him correctly, would commence not with Concrete Experience as with most Experiential Learning Situations, nor with Personal Reflection as in Boot and Boxer's model of Reflective Learning, but with the existing structures of Personal Meaning, or in Personal Construct terms, with the learner's existing construct system. His focus is more explicitly Kellian, his starting point is that learning involves some sort of change in the individual's construct system:

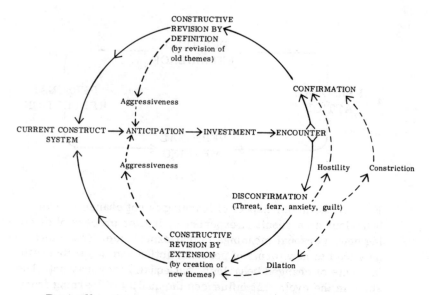

Basically, the model is attempting to represent the ways in which a person's construct system might be elaborated as a result of participation in an experiential learning programme. For those events in the programme for which the person has an adequate construct model, there will be confirmation and the consequent increased definition of the system. For those events for which he has an inadequate model, he will experience 'perturbation' or, in Kellian terms, anxiety, guilt, threat or fear. His response to this disconfirmation may be to act in a hostile or constricting way by converting the disconfirmation into confirmation or ignoring the disconfirmation and thus further define his system. Or he may dilate to seek more data about the disconfirmation in an attempt to re-organise his system or invent new constructs which help him understand the perplexing events. In this case it may well be that he creates new constructs and expands his system. Whether he extends or defines his system, he will have opportunities to test out his new construing aggressively in new situations.

(Beck, 1979, p 6)

This distinction between learning by construction and by reconstruction may be expressed in the following way. Learning by adding new constructs is an elaborative procedure, and involves comparatively little personal threat. As I have mentioned in my discussion of the

Experience Corollary, if we have not encountered a phenomenon before, all that is required is a permeable construct which can subsume this new element, or else a superordinate construct which will permit the inclusion of a new subordinate construct. Reconstruction, on the other hand, has been most fully explored in the field of psychotherapy. If personal construct systems represent our models of reality, and if there is a constant discrepancy between our expectations and the real world, we may handle this in one of several ways. If we are determined to keep our construct systems intact, then no amount of dissonance will dislodge them - we may ignore feedback from the real world which would tend to disconfirm our constructs; we might retreat to a higher level construct so that the incongruity is submerged; we might simply ignore the problem out of existence. Alternatively, acknowledging the apparent mismatch, we might reconstrue, which involves the dismantling of old constructs, and their re-erection into a new framework.

> Miller's work suggests that to construct a more effective plan, the learner must disassemble existing plans, often at many levels of complexity, before recombining them into an alternative structure. He will, as it were, be at some stage caught between plans. Invariably, this leads to sudden and marked drops in performance, a period of depression, uninterest, anxiety, and feelings of hopelessness. At the point where the distance forward is equal to the distance back, there are very strong temptations to reinstate old plans and to reject new methods on the basis that they can be seen not to work. The only solution to this problem is perseverance in the learner and tolerance and support from the trainer.
>
> (Reid, 1977, cit Hopwood and Keen, 1978, p 189)

It seems to me that Rogers, though using slightly different terminology, is referring to the same phenomenon when he writes:

> Learning which involves a change in self-organisation - in the perception of oneself - is threatening and tends to be resisted.
>
> Sometimes these painful and threatening learnings have to do with contradictions with oneself. An example might be the person who believes 'every citizen in this country has equal right to any opportunity which exists'. He also discovers that he has the conviction 'I am unwilling for a Negro to live in my neighbourhood'. Any Learning which arises from this dilemma is

painful and threatening since the two beliefs cannot openly co-exist, and any learning which emerges from the contradiction involves definite change in the structure of self.

(Rogers, 1969, in Entwistle and Hounsell, 1975, p 151)

There is an interesting analogy here with Kuhn's (1970) notion, in science, of paradigm shift, where there may be quite major discontinuities whilst one paradigm is broken down, and reconstructed in a new form. (Nichol, 1980).

CONCLUSION

The purpose of this chapter has been to place Kelly's Personal Construct Theory squarely into the context of adult education. This is thought to be particularly relevant to the purpose of this monograph, because the training of adult educators should epitomise adult education at its best.

In this chapter, I have reviewed several central themes - the concept of lifelong learning, the principle of self-direction, individual differences and their basis in experience, and finally learning from experience. It is not argued that these features are unique to the education of adults, nor that they are the only or even the most significant aspects of adult education. Nonetheless, they are offered as reasonably important issues which are addressed, either implicitly or explicitly, by Kelly's work.

It has been argued that the theory provides a coherent, logical, and internally consistent psychological model of adult cognitive processes, development, and learning. Once a personal construct view of man is accepted, the role of the teacher appears quite unambiguously to be that of facilitator, assisting and intervening in what is, in fact, a natural process of growth, development and construct-system elaboration. And one logical place to begin modelling such teaching practices is in the professional development of adult educators.

EPILOGUE

The training of adult educators, whilst certainly not a new issue, has
rapidly gathered momentum in the past decade or so. If one had to
nominate a particular turning point, it would probably be the final
report of the 1972 UNESCO Conference on Adult Education in Tokyo,
which contained a recommendation about the high priority which should
be given to the training of adult education personnel.

Not only has the dramatic, worldwide increase in demand for adult
education "produced new strains in the patchwork instructional system"
(Grabowski, 1976, p iv) it has also led to an increased demand for
better trained and more educationally sophisticated teachers of adults
in both vocational and non-vocational sectors (Pflüger, 1978, p 12). It
is apparent, however, that courses for the professional development
of adult educators which have been introduced over the years, have
been far from satisfactory.

> Throughout the period under review, and still continuing widely,
> courses tended to purvey practical skills in isolation, and to
> complement these with 'philosophical' or 'inspirational' ele-
> ments. These were series of lectures on general aims and pur-
> poses, or on academic knowledge mostly appropriate to the
> education of children or adolescents, projected at audiences of
> adult educators in the expectation that some of the material
> might be assimilated and would raise levels of skill and morale.
> Later findings showed that such teaching methods rarely did
> more than "widen the chasm between perceived potential in the
> work and unchanging personal practice in its performance", we
> have not yet finished learning from Comenius.
>
> (Elsdon, 1975, p 15)

Many recent studies (for instance, Elsdon, 1975; Campbell, 1977; Clift,
1977 and Pflüger, 1978) whilst making detailed recommendations about
the purposes and content of training programmes for adult education,
are less forthright about methodological issues. This monograph takes
a different approach, in arguing that a particular methodology, in view
of its congruence with significant issues in adult education, might pro-
fitably be employed with a variety of course contents.

In reviewing Kelly's Theory of Personal Constructs, it is clear that he believed we all live in private worlds of meaning, and thus the construction corollary and the individuality corollary inevitably place significant limitations on any teaching approach which relies largely on the direct transmission of material. Indeed, the teacher cannot automatically assume that all people will organise new learning in the same way (or even according to the teacher's own cognitive maps of the subject matter); the organisation corollary sees to that.

In discussing the formal structure of Kelly's theory, I have described the Experience Corollary as the learning corollary. It states: 'a person's construction system varies as he successively construes the replication of events'. This corollary not only points up that each new piece of learning is intimately interconnected with the sum total of the learner's construct system, but it overlays this with the mantle of relativism and individuality - teaching is not so much the passing on of 'established truths', as offering ideas and experiences to be accepted or rejected by the individual learner according to his/her hypotheses and expectations. Because of this intensely personalistic focus, Kelly's theory has been suggested by some as a suitable theoretical substratum for models of adult learning such as those of Knowles, Rogers and Tough.

The Sociality Corollary too, has important implications for understanding and explicating both the dynamics of learning groups and the role of the facilitator of adult learning. It states: 'To the extent that one person construes the construction processes of another, he may play a role in a social process involving the other person'. Learning and teaching in groups is nothing if not a social process, and the clear implication of this corollary is that if someone wants to intervene in the construing processes of another (e.g. in teaching) then he/she must attempt to interpret the interpretive system of the other.

> The person's interpretation need not be accurate, and may be a grossly inaccurate representation of the other person's position, but when he attempts to make some sense of what the other is about, he plays a role in relation to him... one may use one's construction of the other to impede his progress (or to) aid it.
>
> (Bannister and Mair, 1968, p 24)

Teaching, therefore, has as its primary focus, an attempt to understand the construction systems of learners, and Personal Construct Theory has quite positive and inescapable ramifications for teaching and learning at all levels, not least amongst adults. If this is true, then it has significance for the development of adult educators - not only in terms of what they are taught, but equally in terms of how their development is facilitated.

Out of all the mass of literature concerning adult education, there are two consistent research findings which guide my practice. The first is that 'the education of adults involves learning in the context of accumulated experience, skill, knowledge, opinions and prejudices, and building on them as foundations' (Elsdon, 1975, p 6), and the second one is that 'the best resource for adult education is other people' (Salmon, 1979, p 12).

Repertory Grids undoubtedly have enormous potential in equipping individuals with significant insights into their own patterns of thought (construct systems), and I have suggested that this sort of self-knowledge is a necessary, but not sufficient precondition, for effective teaching in adult education. Although learning itself is, and by definition must be, a personal matter, groups play an immensely important role in both the theory and practice of adult education. In relation to Personal Construct Theory, some work carried out by Pope and Shaw, suggests the the immense potential of Repertory Grid Technique in exploring shared and individual structures of meaning within groups.

It is important to state that I am not claiming that Repertory Grid Technique could conceivably provide a self-contained approach to the development of teachers in adult education. What I do claim, however, is that it can provide a logically consistent, intellectually appealing, and excitingly innovative way of supplementing and rendering more personally relevant, the offerings presently available in programmes for the professional development of adult educators. And, what is more, as soon as someone implements an approach to education which draws on personal construct theory, he/she is, by that very fact, moving significantly towards greater learner-centredness.

Throughout this monograph, I have tried to show that although Personal Construct Theory is far more than a theory of learning, there are nonetheless far-reaching implications for education, in adopting a Kellian view of 'man-the-scientist'. Kelly's theory is at once a sophisticated cognitive psychology and a personality theory, as well as giving insights into social psychology (e. g. teacher/learner interaction or group processes) and the relations of language and thought (psycholinguistics). Its implications for educational practice are manifold and, despite its inadequacies, it seems to me the most complete and convincing statement we have at present to account for many of the complexities of human behaviour, and it offers simultaneously, both a philosophy and a technology to enhance the training of teachers in general, and of adult educators in particular.

APPENDIX

THE FORMAL STRUCTURE OF PERSONAL CONSTRUCT THEORY

The essence of Kelly's theory is contained in a single fundamental postulate; 'That a person's processes are psychologically channelised by the ways in which he anticipates events'.

This proposition is carefully worded, and its properties are discussed at length by Bannister and Mair (1968). Essentially, it rests on the assumption that we all seek to make sense out of the world around us, and to do so, construct more or less elaborate, multi-dimensional models of reality inside our heads. When something actually happens, we try to fit it into our system or constructs, and if it does not fit, we either develop a new (or revised) construct to handle that experience, or we modify our perception of the experience to fit with what we were expecting. The idea of channelising is important, because Kelly suggested that every person, place, event or idea could be put some- where along a series of intersecting continua, which uniquely fixes its location and personal meaning. Bannister and Mair comment:

It is assumed from the start that a person's processes are psychologically channelised by means of a network of pathways and do not float about in an uncharted emptiness. The network of channels is presumed to be flexible and modifiable, but it is structured and both facilitates and restricts a person's range of action. These channels are erected as ways, or means to an end, that end being the anticipation of events. Kelly is not concerned primarily with any ideal ways of anticipating events, but the ways in which individual men choose and devise to antici- pate the events of which they are aware. Different people may anticipate different events and formulate different modes for anticipating similar events.

(Bannister and Mair, 1968, pp 12/13)

Kelly's basic tenet is supported and elaborated by eleven Corollaries, as follows. (These explanations draw heavily upon material in Bannister and Fransella 1971, and Bannister and Mair 1968):

1   Construction Corollary: A person anticipates events by construing their replications.

In the continuous onrush of daily events, a person notes similarities and differences, in order to predict when a replication will
occur. All constructs are necessarily bi-polar in that, for
example, a person cannot be seen as intelligent, without this
implying not only some similarity between this person and
certain other people, but a contrast with other, stupid, people.
Because events are never precisely the same, the anticipation
of replication involves looking for underlying themes or abstract
similarities, and Kelly used this as an indication of the fallacy
of Stimulus-Response psychology. Instead of responding to a
stimulus, in fact people respond to what they perceive to be a
stimulus, which is in turn a function of the kind of replications
imposed on (detected in) their universe. Kelly often used the
analogy of listening to music to illustrate this corollary, and
this is supported by Humphrey (1933) who showed that it is
possible to condition a man to withdraw his hand when the letter
'G' is played on the piano and accompanied by an electric shock.
However, the subject fails to twitch at all during a rendition of
'Home Sweet Home', despite the fact that the tune contains the
note 'G' fourteen times, presumably because he construes it as
a tune, and not as a series of notes.

2   Individuality Corollary: Persons differ from each other in their
construction of events.

Put simply, this corollary means that there are individual differences, and that different individuals are likely to place
rather different interpretations on the same events and to set up
rather different constructions to subsume the different sets of
events which impinge on them. It has intrigued psychologists
for years, why two people in the same situation behave differently. Kelly's answer is that they are not in the same situation, it
is only the 'same' from the perspective of a third person. Kelly
was careful never to say that no two people could ever have
exactly the same constructs, organised in exactly the same way,
but in practice the likelihood of two people seeing the world in
identical terms is infinitesimal, and for all practical purposes
we can argue that each of us lives in a unique world.

3   Organisation Corollary: Each person characteristically evolves, for his convenience in anticipating events, a construction system embracing ordinal relationships between constructs.

If a person develops a set of constructs to help in anticipating events and ordering his world, unless some form of organisation is brought to bear, he will be trapped in repeated confusion and uncertainty because different construct sets yield contradictory or unrelated predictions. Kelly therefore suggests that each person characteristically sets up personal hierarchical systems of constructs, where some constructs are higher or more superordinate. This is analogous to the notion of class inclusion from traditional logic (e.g. the class 'furniture' subsumes chair, couch, table, wardrobe, etc.) but since constructs are bi-polar, it is not identical to the traditional notion. One often-quoted example is the fact that 'good-bad' for many people is a higher order construct, that typically subsumes many other constructs at least in part. 'Good' for instance may be highly related to 'kind', 'intelligent', or 'religious' and 'bad' to their psychological opposites. When eliciting constructs from people, there is a tendency for them to slip from one level of abstraction to the next, without being aware of it, or to offer one construct pair, and then to rank items or events according to a higher order construct.

4   Dichotomy Corollary: A person's construction system is composed of a finite number of dichotomous constructs.

Because it is not possible, logically, to affirm something without, at the same time, denying something else, constructs are usually seen as bi-polar, and this distinguishes them from 'concepts', which we can define as single notions. So a person's construct system comprises a finite number of these bi-polar constructs, which are organised hierarchically, and abstractly cross-referenced by the user. No-one's thinking, however, is completely fluid, and no-one has an infinite number of pathways along which their thinking may proceed. The idea that constructs are dichotomous, black-white, affairs, at first sight seems to deny the sort of relativism in thinking which the sophisticated and the liberal demand; Kelly however insists that there is nothing categorical about a construct:

> Neither our constructs nor our construing systems come to us from nature, except, of course, from our own

nature, It must be noted that this philosophical position of constructive alternativism has much more powerful epistemological implications than one might at first suppose. We cannot say that constructs are essences distilled by the mind out of available reality. They are imposed upon events, not abstracted from them. There is only one place they come from; and that is from the person who is to use them. He devises them. Moreover, they do not stand for anything or represent anything as a symbol, for example, is supposed to do.

So what are they? They are reference axes, upon which one may project events in an effort to make sense out of what is going on. In this sense, they are like cartesian co-ordinates, the x, y and z axes of analytic geometry. Events correspond to the points plotted within cartesian space. We can locate the points and express relations between points by specifying x, y and z distances. The cartesian axes do not represent the points projected upon them, but serve as guidelines for locating those points. That, also, is what constructs do for events, including ones that have not yet occurred. They help us to locate them, understand them and anticipate them.

But we must not take the cartesian analogy too literally. Descartes's axes were lines or scales, each containing in order, an infinite number of imaginary points. Certainly his x or y axis embodied well enough the notion of shadings or a succession of greys. Yet a construct is not quite such an axis.

A construct is the basic contrast between two groups. When it is imposed it serves both to distinguish between its elements and to group them. Thus the construct refers to the nature of the distinction one attempts to make between events, not to the array in which his events appear to stand when he gets through applying the distinction between them and all the others.

Suppose one is dealing with the construct of good versus bad. Such a construct is not a representation of all things that are good, and an implicit exclusion of all that are

bad. Nor is it a representation of all that are bad. It is
not even a representation of all things that can be called
either good or bad. The construct, of itself, is the kind
of contrast one perceives and not in any way a representation of objects. As far as the construct is concerned,
there is no good-better-best scale, or any bad-worse-
worst array.

But whilst constructs do not represent or symbolise
events, they do enable us to cope with events, which is
a statement of quite a different order. They also enable
us to put events into arrays or scales, if we wish.
Suppose, for example, we apply our construct to elements, say persons, or to their acts. Consider three
persons. One may make a good-bad distinction between
them which will say that two of them are good in relation
to the third, and that the third is bad in relation to the
two good ones. Then he may, in turn, apply his construct
between the two good ones and say one of them is good
with respect to the other formerly 'good' one and the
one already labelled 'bad'.

This, of course, makes one of the persons, or acts,
good in terms of one cleavage that has been made and
bad in relation to the other. But this relativism applies
only to the objects; the construct of good versus bad is
itself absolute.

(Kelly, 1966)

5   Choice Corollary: A person chooses for himself that alternative
in a dichotomised construct through which he anticipates the
greater possibility for the elaboration of his system.

In many ways, this corollary may be seen as central to Kelly's
theory, because it pinpoints the process through which behaviour
is produced, and at the same time gives to man his essential
directionality. In any given situation, a person has the alternative of choosing that interpretation which seems to offer a clearer
sight of the things that he already knows, or a base from which
to strike out towards unexplored possibilities. Kelly writes:

Here is where inner turmoil so frequently manifests
itself. Which shall a man choose, security or adventure?

> Shall he choose that which may eventually give him a
> wider understanding? For the man of constricted outlook
> whose world begins to crumble, death may appear to
> provide the only immediate certainty which he can lay
> hands on.
>
> (Kelly, 1966)

It is worth noting that a person does not necessarily or consistently choose the alternative which in any 'objective' sense will lead to the clearest definition or the most extensive elaboration of his system. His choice is clearly governed by his own awareness of the possibilities involved, It was on this sort of reasoning that Holland (1970) based his criticism, that this corollary is untestable and therefore not scientific. However, this has been countered by Bannister, amongst others, who claims that it is testable, if we are able to know enough about the structure of a particular individual's system, to predict his choices in terms of that system. It could be argued, therefore, that whatever his choice may be, either for constricted certainty or for broadened understanding, every decision is essentially elaborative - 'to our way of thinking, there is a continuing movement toward the anticipation of events, rather than a series of barters for temporal satisfactions and this movement is the essence of human life itself.' (Kelly, 1955, p 68)

6   Range Corollary: A construct is convenient for the anticipation of a finite range of events only.

Kelly uses the term 'focus of convenience' to indicate those things for which a construct was specifically developed by its user. Since (as I have already mentioned) a construct system includes a finite number of constructs, so a construct system, subsystem or specific construct dimension has only a limited range of utility or applicability - a simple example is that the construct 'black-white' cannot be applied to a red tomato. Unlike a concept, which is said to embrace all elements which are similar in some particular respect, a construct is not a class, or an abstraction of a class, but a dichotomous reference axis. Thus it may be said to have a focus of convenience (a set of events which its user finds can be most conveniently ordered within its context) and a range of convenience (a broader set of events which the construct can deal with, if sometimes less effectively) and a further set of events in relation to which it is useless; see, for instance, Brown's (1958) question 'Is a boulder sweet or sour?' It is also worth noting here that the words used to specify the poles of a construct should not be confused with the constructive distinction which they are intended to represent. Thus two people may use the same words and yet have in mind a rather different similarity-contrast dimension, or alternatively use different words, when they have in mind much the same distinction. The focus and range of convenience needs to be negotiated, to discover what similarities, if any, exist between different people's construct systems.

7   Experience Corollary: A person's construction system varies as he successively construes the replication of events.

Since the fundamental postulate argues that man is concerned essentially with the anticipation of events, it becomes necessary to suppose that as events unfold and his predictions turn out for better or for worse, his construct system will vary to incorporate some aspects of the new evidence - indeed one manifestation of a malfunctioning individual is where events consistently disconfirm the predictions, yet no change is made in the construct system, with the result that it becomes progressively less realistic.

This corollary is the learning corollary, but from the foregoing it should be clear that Kelly sees learning as taking place all the time, and being so general that it need not be elevated into an area of study in its own right.

> The burden of our assumption is that learning is not a special class of psychological processes; it is synonymous with any and all psychological processes. It is not something that happens to a person on occasion; it is what makes him a person in the first place.
>
> (Kelly, 1955, p 75)

Indeed, familiar learning experiments take on a new perspective, when viewed in Personal Construct terms:

> He (the respondent) too directs his psychological processes by seeking the recurrent theme in the experiment. If he segments the experience into separate trials and then further separates the trials into reinforced trials

and unreinforced trials, he may hear the same repetitive
theme which the experimenter hears. On the other hand,
he may not be so conventional. He may listen for other
kinds of themes he has heard before. He may not even
segment his experience into the kinds of trials or events
the experimenter expects. In the language of music, he
may employ another way of 'phrasing'. Viewed in this
manner, the problem of learning is not merely one of
determining how many, or even what kinds of, reinforce-
ments fix a response, or how many non-reinforcements
extinguish it, but rather, how does the subject 'phrase'
the experience, what recurrent themes does he hear,
what movements does he define, and what validation of
his predictions does he reap? When a subject fails to
meet the experimenter's expectations, it may be inappro-
priate to say that 'he has not learned'; rather one might
say that what the subject learned was not what the experimenter expected him to learn. If we are to have a pro-
ductive science of psychology, let us put the burden of
discovery on the experimenter rather than on the subject.
Let the experimenter find out what the subject is thinking
about, rather than asking the subject to find out what the
experimenter is thinking about.

(Kelly, 1955, pp 76/7)

8   Modulation Corollary: The variation in a person's construction
system is limited by the permeability of the constructs within
whose range of convenience the variants lie.

In this context, permeability means openness to the inclusion of
new elements, or in the case of a superordinate construct, to
the inclusion of new subordinate constructs. Since this corollary
is concerned with change, and Kelly defines man as a form of
perpetual motion, then it could be expected that construct systems in healthy individuals would be constantly varied and
modified. Kelly buttresses this point when he mentions that in
psychotherapeutic situations, people are often troubled by an
inability to construe new events, or to reconstrue old events in
a way which would enhance their adjustment, they have encountered some impermeability in their construct system. Unless an
individual has, or can develop, a higher order construct to subsume a newly created construct, it runs the risk of standing out
in isolation, and thus being difficult for the person to use as a
consistent reference axis.

9 Fragmentation Corollary: A person may successively employ a
   variety of construction subsystems which are inferentially
   incompatible with each other.

Though the notion that constructs are organised is an important
part of Kelly's theory, it is possible for various constructs to be
related to one another in flexible ways, which enhances the
capacity of the construct system to be used creatively. Furthermore, very few people, if any, achieve completely internally
consistent construct systems, with every construct logically
related and implied by every other one. One explanation for this
phenomenon is that people are simply unaware of the inconsis-
tencies in their construct systems, or even that their awareness
is suppressed, thus allowing them to go on using incompatible
constructs side by side. The other main explanation, and one
which is very likely in many cases, is that there is some superordinate construct in use, of which the outside observer is
unaware. Bannister and Mair give the following example:

> A parent may hug and kiss a child at one moment,
> smack him a little later, and shortly afterwards ignore
> him when he insists on showing off by excessive chatter-
> ing. To the casual observer, it may seem that one
> reponse could not be anticipated from the previous one
> and that grossly inconsistent behaviour and constructions
> were being adopted by the parent. This may be the case,
> but need not be so... When, for example, the parent's
> superordinate constructs concerning love and training
> are considered, some thread of consistency in the
> various actions may be noted.
>
> (Bannister and Mair, 1968, p 22)

10 Commonality Corollary: To the extent that one person employs
    a construction of experience which is similar to that employed
    by another, his processes are psychologically similar to those
    of the other person.

This is the obverse of the Individuality Corollary, and stresses
that people are not similar because they have experienced
similar events, but because they construe - ie discriminate,
interpret, see the implications of events - in similar ways. In
other words, the point is that having encountered different sets
of circumstances, and worked out what these circumstances
were all about, people have come to similar conclusions. It is,

of course, extremely dangerous to assume, on the basis of a
temporary similarity of this nature, that people will continue to
be alike in future. This corollary sheds some light on the age
old conundrum as to whether it is shared experiences which
draw people together - Kelly's response would surely be that
similar perspectives (construct systems) cause people to be
more alike (psychologically) then shared experiences per se.

11   Sociality Corollary: To the extent that one person construes the
construction processes of another, he may play a role in a
social process involving the other person.

This corollary is the only one which concerns itself overtly with
the social processes, and interpersonal interaction and understanding. It bears a close relation to what is popularly called
role taking, because it requires an attempt to enter the construct
system of another person, and

> this subtly places a demand upon him, one he cannot
> lightly reject, if his own experience is to be completed.
> He must put himself tentatively in the other person's
> shoes. Only by enacting that role can he sense the impact
> of what happens as a result of taking the point of view he
> thinks his friend must have.
>
> (Kelly, 1966)

Clearly this corollary has important implications, both for
social interactions (including teaching) and for therapeutic
situations; it involves more than merely observing the other's
behaviour, but attempting actively to construe the construction
processes of the other. How well or how badly this venture is
undertaken is immaterial, for it generates dialogue about
personally significant matters, and ultimately leads to a better
shared understanding of each person's construct system.

REFERENCES

ADAMS, R.S. and BIDDLE, B.J. Realities of Teaching; Explorations with video tape, Holt, New York, 1970

ADAMS-WEBBER, J. 'Elicited versus provided constructs in repertory grid technique: a review, 'British Journal of Medical Psychology, 61, 1970 pp 83-90.

ADAMS-WEBBER, J.R. Personal Construct Theory: Concepts and Applications, John Wiley and Sons, Toronto, 1979

ANDERSON, J. 'Informal Adult Education in the Classical World', in Powell, A. (ed) Adult Education Papers and Abstracts, Department of Adult Education, University of Manchester, 1974

APPS, J.W. Toward a Working Philosophy of Adult Education, Occasional Paper No. 36, Syracuse University, Syracuse, New York, 1973

APPS J.W. and BOYD, R.D. 'A Conceptual Model for Adult Education', Unpublished paper, University of Wisconin, Madison, 1976

ARGYRIS, C. and SCHON, D.A. Theory in Practice: Increasing Professional Effectiveness, Jossey Bass, San Francisco, 1974

BANDURA, A. Social Learning Theory, Prentice-Hall, Englewood Cliffs, New Jersey, 1977

BANNISTER, D. (ed) Perspectives in Personal Construct Theory, Academic Press, London, 1970

BANNISTER, D. (ed) New Perspectives in Personal Construct Theory, Academic Press, London, 1977

BANNISTER, D. Notes for the Opening Panel Discussion, Third International Congress on Personal Construct Psychology, Breukelen, July 1979

BANNISTER, D. and FRANSELLA, F. Inquiring Man: The Theory of Personal Constructs, Penguin, Harmondsworth, Middlesex, 1971

BANNISTER, D. and MAIR, J.M.M. The Evaluation of Personal Constructs, Academic Press, London, 1968

BECK, J.E. 'Changing Construing by Experiential Learning Methods - A Framework for Research', Paper presented at the Third International Congress on Personal Construct Psychology, Breukelen, July 1979.

BENNETT, N. Teaching Styles and Pupil Progress, Open Books London, 1976

BERGER, P.L. and LUCKMAN, T. The Social Construction of Reality, Penguin, London, 1966

BERNSTEIN, B. 'On the classification and framing of educational knowledge', Class Codes and Control, Volume 1, Theoretical Studies Towards A Sociology of Language, Routledge and Kegan Paul, London, 1971

BIGGE, M.L. Learning Theories for Teachers, Harper and Row, New York, 1971

BISSELL, J.S. Book Review of Bennett's 'Teaching Styles and Pupil Progress', in Harvard Educational Review Vol. 47, No. 2, May 1977, pp 214-222

BLOOM, B.S. et al. Taxonomy of Educational Objectives - Handbook 1: Cognitive Domain, McKay, New York, 1956

BONARIUS, J.C.J. 'Research in the Personal Construct Theory of George A. Kelly: Role Construct Repertory Test and Basic Theory', in Maher, B. (ed) Progress in Experimental Personality Research, Vol. 2, Academic Press, London, 1965

BOOT, R.L. 'A Guide to the Methods of the Management Learning Project', mimeo, London Business School, Feb. 1979

BOOT, R.L. and BOXER, P. 'Reflective Learning', A paper presented at the Conference 'Advances in Management Education', UMIST, Manchester, April 1979

BOYDELL, T.H. 'Experiential Learning', Manchester Monograph No. 5, Department of Adult Education, University of Manchester, 1976

BRUNDAGE, D.H. and MACKERACHER, D. Adult Learning Principles and their Application to Program Planning, Ministry of Education, Ontario, Toronto, 1980

CAMPBELL, D.D. Adult Education as a Field of Study and Practice: Strategies for Development, Centre for Continuing Education, University of British Columbia, Vancouver, 1977

CANDY, P. C. A Personal Construct Approach to Adult Learning, Adelaide College of the Arts and Education, Adelaide, 1980

CAWLEY, R. W. V., MILLER, S. A., and MILLIGAN, J. N. 'Cognitive Style and the Adult Learner', Adult Education, Vol. XXVI, No. 2, 1976, pp 101-116

CENTRE FOR EDUCATIONAL RESEARCH AND INNOVATION Recurrent Education: A Strategy for Lifelong Learning, O. E. C. D., Paris, 1973

CHAMBERLAIN, M. N. 'The Competencies of Adult Educators', Adult Education Vol XI No. 2, 1961

CLARK, R. P. and NISBET, J. D. 'The First Two Years of Teaching', mimeo, Aberdeen College of Education, 1963

CLIFT, J. C. (Chairman) Report of a Working Party on Training of Continuing Educators, National Council of Adult Education, Wellington, New Zealand, March 1977.

COVE, M. 'A View of Teacher Self Evaluation', Paper Presented at Schools Commission Conference on In-Service Education, Leura, New South Wales, November 1974

CRAIK, G. L. The Pursuit of Knowledge Under Difficulties, Bell and Daldy, London, rev. ed. 1866

CROPLEY, A. J. Lifelong Education: a psychological analysis, Pergamon Press/UNESCO, Oxford 1977

CROPLEY, A. J. and DAVE, R. H. Lifelong Education and the Training of Teachers, Pergamon Press and UNESCO Institute of Education, Paris and Hamburg, 1978

CROSS, K. P. Accent on Learning, Jossey-Bass, San Fransisco, 1976

DANIEL, J. S. 'Learning Styles and Strategies; the Work of Gordon Pask', in Entwistle and Hounsell, op. cit, 1975

DAVE, R. H. 'Lifelong Education and the School Curriculum,' UIE Monograph No. 1, UNESCO Institute for Education, Hamburg, 1973

DAVE, R. H. (ed) Foundations of Lifelong Education, Pergamon Press/ UNESCO, Oxford 1976

DE BONO, E. Wordpower, Penguin Books, Harmondsworth, Middlesex, 1979

DEWEY, J. Democracy and Education, Macmillan, New York, 1916

DUFF, B. Transactional Analysis for Teachers, International Transactional Analysis Association, Berkeley, California, 1972

DUKE, C. Australian Perspectives on Lifelong Education, Australian Council for Educational Research, Hawthorn, 1976

DUNKIN, M. J. and BIDDLE, B. J. The Study of Teaching, Holt Rinehart and Winston, New York, 1974

ELSDON, K. T. Training for Adult Education, Nottingham Studies in the Theory and Practice of the Education of Adults, Department of Adult Education, University of Nottingham and the National Institute of Adult Education, 1975

ENTWISTLE, N. and HANLEY, M. 'Personality, Cognitive Style and Students' Learning Strategies', Higher Education Bulletin, Vol. 6, No. 1, Winter 1977/8, University of Lancaster Institute for Post-Compulsory Education

ENTWISTLE, N. and HOUNSELL, D. 'How Students Learn', Readings in Higher Education 1, Institute for Research and Development in Post Compulsory Education, University of Lancaster, 1975

FAURE, E. (ed) Learning to Be: the World of Education Today and Tomorrow, UNESCO, Paris, 1972

FRANCIS, R. 'The Integration of Theory and Practice: A Freirian Analysis of the Concurrency Model', Unpublished paper, University of New England, Armidale, 1980

FRANSELLA, F. (ed) Personal Construct Psychology 1977: Papers Presented at the Second International Congress on Personal Construct Theory held at Oxford in July 1977, Academic Press, London, 1978

FRANSELLA, F. and BANNISTER, D. A Manual for Repertory Grid Technique, Academic Press, London, 1977

FREIRE, P. Pedagogy of the Oppressed, Penguin, Harmondsworth, Middlesex, 1972

FREUD, A. (trans. B. Low) 'The Relation Between Psychoanalysis and Pedagogy', in Psychoanalysis for Teachers and Parents, Beacon Press, Boston, 1960

GAGE, N. L. 'Paradigms for Research on Teaching', in Gage, N. L. (ed) Handbook of Research on Teaching, American Educational Research Association, Rand McNally, Chicago, 1963

GAGE, N. L. Teacher Effectiveness and Teacher Education, Pacific Books, Palo Alto, California, 1972

GAGNÉ, R. M. The Conditions of Learning, Holt Rinehart and Winston, New York, 1970

GALLAGHER, J. J. 'Three Studies of the Classroom', in Gallagher J. J. et al (eds) 'Classroom Observation', American Educational Research Association Monograph Series on Curriculum Evaluation, Monograph No. 6, Rand McNally, Chicago, 1970

GLANVILLE, R. 'Constriction by Diction, Construing by Doing', Workshop and Paper presented at Third International Congress on Personal Construct Psychology, Breukelen, July 1979

GOBLE, N. M. and PORTER, J. F. 'The Changing Role of the Teacher', IBE Studies in Comparative Education, UNESCO, Hamburg, 1977

GRABOWSKI, S. M. 'Training Teachers of Adults: Models and Innovative Programs', Syracuse University Publications in Continuing Education, Occasional Paper No. 46, National Association for Public, Continuing and Adult Education, New York, 1976

HARRI-AUGSTEIN, E. S. 'Reflecting on Structures of Meaning: A Process of Learning-to-Learn', in Fransella, op. cit, 1978

HILGARD, E. R. and BOWER, G. H. Theories of Learning, Appleton-Century-Crofts, New York, 1966

HINKLE, D. N. 'The Change of Personal Constructs from the viewpoint of a Theory of Construct Implications', Unpublished Ph. D. thesis, Ohio State University, 1965. (A convenient summary is given in Bannister and Mair op. cit 1968 and Fransella and Bannister op. cit 1977)

HOBART, R. B. 'Towards an Integrated System of TAFE Teacher Education', in Philosophies, Programmes and Possibilities - Proceedings of a Planning Conference 29 Sept - 1 Oct 1979, Department of Technical and Further Education, Adelaide College of the Arts and Education, Adelaide, 1979

HOLE, J. Essay on the History and Management of Literary, Scientific and Mechanics Institutions in England, London 1853

HOLLAND, R. 'George Kelly: constructive innocent and reluctant existentialist', in Bannister, D. (ed) op. cit. 1970

HOPWOOD, W. and KEEN, T. 'TARGET: A New Approach to the Appraisal of Teaching', Programmed Learning and Educational Technology, Vol. 15, No. 3, August 1978, pp 187-195

HOULE, C.O. In Proceedings of the Fifth Leadership Conference for University Adult Educators, Centre for the Study of Liberal Education for Adults, Chicago, 1957 (in Campbell, op.cit, 1977.)

HUDSON, L. Contrary Imaginations: A Psychological Study of the Young Student, Penguin, Harmondsworth, Middlesex, 1967

HUNT, D.E. Matching Models in Education: The Co-ordination of Teaching Methods with Student Characteristics, Ontario Institute for Studies in Education, Toronto, 1971

ILLICH, I. and VERNE, E. Imprisoned in the Global Classroom, Writers and Readers Publishing Co-operative, London, 1976

INDUSTRIAL TRAINING RESEARCH UNIT What's in a Style?... Measuring the Effectiveness of Instruction, Cambridge, 1975

IRELAND, D.S. et al A report on a Training Programme for Teachers in Curriculum Development Skills, Ontario Institute for Studies in Education, Ottawa Valley Section, Ottawa, 1971

JACKSON, P.W. Life in Classrooms, Holt, New York, 1968

JAMES, W. The Principles of Psychology, Holt, New York, 1890

JESSUP, F.W. Lifelong Learning: A Symposium on Continuing Education, Pergamon Press, Oxford, 1969

JENSEN, G., LIVERIGHT, A.A. and HALLENBECK, W. (eds) Adult Education: An Emerging Field of University Study, Adult Education Association of USA, 1964

JOYCE, B.R. and HAROOTUNIAN, B. 'Teaching as Problem Solving', Journal of Teacher Education, Vol. XV, No. 4, Dec. 1964, pp 420-427

JOYCE, B. and WEIL, M. Models of Teaching, Prentice Hall, New Jersey, 1972

KELLY, G.A. The Psychology of Personal Constructs Vols. 1 and 2, Norton, New York, 1955

KELLY, G.A. 'A Brief Introduction to Personal Construct Theory', unpublished manuscript, Brandeis University, 1966 (cit. Bannister and Mair op.cit. 1968)

KELLY, G.A. 'The Role of Classification in Personality Theory' in Maher, B. (ed) Clinical Psychology and personality: the selected papers of George Kelly, Wiley, New York, 1969

KIDD, J.R. How Adults Learn, Association Press, New York, 1974

KINGSLEY, H.L. and GARRY, R. The Nature and Conditions of Learning, Prentice Hall, Englewood Cliffs, New Jersey, 2nd ed., 1957

KNOWLES, M.S. The Modern Practice of Adult Education: Andragogy versus Pedagogy, Association Press, New York, 1970

KNOWLES, M.S. 'Self Directing Enquiry: Innovations in Teaching Styles and Approaches Based upon Adult Learning', in Journal of Education for Social Work, Vol. 8, No. 2, Spring 1972.

KNOWLES, M.S. The Adult Learner: A Neglected Species, Gulf Publishing, Houston, 1973

KNOWLES, M.S. Self-Directed Learning: a guide for learners and teachers, Association Press, New York, 1975

KNOWLES, M.S. 'Emerging Ideas in Adult Education', Transcript of Tape recorded Seminar held at Adelaide, 31st July 1978. Department of Further Education, South Australia, October 1978

KNOX, A.B. Adult Development and Learning, Jossey-Bass, San Francisco, 1977

KOLB, D.A. Learning Style Inventory Technical Manual, McBer and Co., Boston, 1976a

KOLB, D.A. 'Management and the Learning Process', California Management Review, Vol. XVIII No. 3, Spring 1976, pp 21-31. 1976b

KOLB, D.A., RUBIN, I. and McINTYRE, J. Organisational Psychology: An Experiential Approach, Prentice Hall, Englewood Cliffs, New Jersey, 1971

KUHN, T.S. The Structure of Scientific Revolutions, University of Chicago Press, 2nd ed., 1970

LENGRAND, P. An Introduction to Lifelong Education, UNESCO, Paris, 1970

98

LIFSHITZ, M. 'Quality Professionals: Does Training Make a Difference? A Personal Construct Theory Study of the Issue', British Journal of Social and Clinical Psychology, No. 13, 1974, pp 183-9

LIVINGSTONE, SIR R. The Future in Education, Cambridge University Press, Cambridge 1941

McDONALD, F.J. 'The Influence of Learning Theories on Education', in Hilgard, E.R. (ed) Theories of Learning and Instruction, 63rd Year Book of National Society for the Study of Education Part 1, University of Chicago Press, 1964

MARTON, F. 'What Does It Take to Learn?' Paper presented at the symposium on Strategies for Research and Development in Higher Education, University of Gothenburg, 7th-12th September 1975, in Entwistle and Hounsell, op.cit, 1975

MASLOW, A.H. The Farther Reaches of Human Nature, Penguin, Harmondsworth, Middlesex, 1973

MEDLEY, D.M. and MITZEL, H.E. 'Measuring Classroom Behaviour by Systematic Observation' in Gage, N.L. (ed), op.cit. 1963

MINISTRY OF RECONSTRUCTION Final Report of the Adult Education Committee, HMSO, London, 1919

MORRIS, B. Objectives and Perspectives in Education: Studies in Educational Theory 1955-70, Routledge and Kegan Paul, New York, 1972

MORRISON, A. and McINTYRE, D. Teachers and Teaching, Penguin, Harmondsworth, Middlesex, 1969

MULFORD, W.R. 'Andragogy and some implications for Teacher Educators', in Mulford W et al, A.C.T. Papers on Education 1978-9, Canberra College of Advanced Education, Canberra, 1979

MURPHY, P.D. and BROWN, M.M., 'Conceptual Systems and Teaching Styles', American Educational Research Journal 7, 1970, pp 529-540

NEIMEYER, R.A. 'The Structure and Meaningfulness of Tacit Construing', Paper Presented at the Third International Congress on Personal Construct Psychology, Breukelen, July 1979.

NICHOL, J.B. 'Makers of Realities: A Theory of Paradigm Transition Learning', unpublished paper, University of Manchester Department of Adult and Higher Education, 1980

OHLIGER, J.D. 'Is Lifelong Education a Guarantee of Permanent Inadequacy?' Convergence, Vol VII, No. 2, 1974, pp 47-58

ORNSTEIN, R. The Psychology of Consciousness, W.H. Freeman, San Francisco, 1975

PARKYN, G.W. Towards a Conceptual Model of Lifelong Education, UNESCO, Educational Studies and Documents, New Series No 12, Paris, 1973

PASK, G. 'Conversational techniques in the study and practice of education', British Journal of Educational Psychology, 46, 1976, pp 1-154.

PASK, G., KALLIKOURDIS, D. and SCOTT, B.C.E. 'The Representation of Knowables', International Journal of Man-Machine Studies 7, 1975, pp 14-134.

PASK, G., and SCOTT, B.C.E. 'Caste: A System for Exhibiting Learning Strategies and Regulating Uncertainties,' International Journal of Man-Machine Studies 5, 1973, pp 17-52.

PASK, G., and SCOTT, B.C.E. 'Learning Strategies and Individual Competence', International Journal of Man-Machine Studies 4, 1972, pp 217-253.

PASK, G., SCOTT, B.C.E. and KALLIKOURDIS, D. 'The Theory of Conversations and Individuals', International Journal of Man-Machine Studies 5, 1973, pp 443-566.

PERROTT, E. et al 'An investigation into teachers' reactions to a self-instructional microteaching course,' Programmed Learning and Educational Technology, Vol 13, No 2, 1976, pp 25-35.

PFLÜGER, A. The Training and Retraining of Adult Educators - Consolidated Report of a Group of Experts, Council of Europe, Strasbourg, 1978

PITTENGER, O.E. and GOODING, C.T. Learning Theories in Educational Practice: An Integration of Psychological Theory and Educational Philosophy, John Wiley, New York, 1971

POLANYI, M. Personal Knowledge: Towards a Post-Critical Philosophy, Routledge and Kegan Paul, London, 1962

POLANYI, M. The Tacit Dimension, Doubleday, Garden City, New York, 1967

POPE, M. 'Monitoring and Reflecting in Teacher Training' in Fransella, F. (ed), op. cit, 1978

POPE, M. and SHAW, M. L. G. 'Negotiation in Learning', Paper Presented at the Third International Congress on Personal Construct Psychology, Breukelen, July 1979.

POSTMAN, N. and WEINGARTNER, C. Teaching as a Subversive Activity, Penguin, Harmondsworth, Middlesex, 1971

RAYWID, M. A. 'Models of the Teaching-Learning Situation', Phi Delta Kappan, Vol. 58, No 8, April 1977, pp 631-5.

REID, F. 'A Preliminary evaluation of the advanced learning and reading course', Assessment in Higher Education Vol 2, No. 1, 1977, pp 5-30.

REESE, H. W. and OVERTON, W. F. 'Models of Development and Theories of Development' in Goulet, L. R. and Baltes, P. B. (eds) Life-Span Developmental Psychology, Academic Press, New York, 1970

ROBERTSON, J. D. C. 'An analysis of the views of supervisors on the attributes of successful student teachers', British Journal of Educational Psychology, Vol. 32, 1957, pp 275-91.

RODRIGUEZ, C. 'Lifelong Education', Educational Documentation and Information: Bulletin of the International Bureau of Education, 46th Year, No. 185, UNESCO, Geneva, 1972

ROGERS, C. Freedom to Learn, Merrill, Columbus, Ohio, 1969

RUDDOCK, R. 'Sociological Perspectives on Adult Education', Manchester Monograph No. 2, Department of Adult Education, University of Manchester, 1972

RUNKEL, P. J. 'A brief model for pupil-teacher interaction' in Gage, N. L. (ed) op. cit, 1963

RYLE, A. Frames and Cages: The Repertory Grid Approach to Human Understanding, University of Sussex Press, London, 1975.

RYCHLAK, J. F. The Psychology of Rigorous Humanism, John Wiley and Sons, New York, 1977

RYTOVAARA, M. 'Some Applications of PCT in Supervision', Paper Presented at the Third International Congress on Personal Construct Psychology, Breukelen, July 1979

SALMON, P. W. 'A Model of the Adult Learning Process', Unpublished paper, University of Melbourne, Agricultural Extension Research Unit, 1979

SHAW, M. L. G. 'Interactive Computer Programs for Eliciting Personal Models of the World', In Fransella, F. (ed) op.cit, 1978

SHAW, M. L. G. and THOMAS, L. F. 'FOCUS on Education', International Journal of Man-Machine Studies, 10, 1978, pp 139-173.

SIMON, A. and BOYER, E.G. (eds) Mirrors for Behaviour: an anthology of classroom observation instruments, Vols. 1-14, Philadelphia, 1967-1970

SOLOMON, D., BEZDEK, W.E., and ROSENBERG, L. Teaching Styles and Learning, Centre for the Study of Liberal Education for Adults, Research Report. Chicago, Illinois, 1963

SRINIVASAN, L. Perspectives on Non Formal Adult Learning, World Education, New York, 1977

STOLUROW, L. M. 'Model the Master Teacher or Master the Teaching Model', in Stones and Morris, op.cit. 1972

STONES, E. and MORRIS, S. Teaching Practice: Problems and Perspectives, Methuen, London, 1972

SUTTON, C. 'Theory in the Classroom' British Journal of Teacher Education, Vol. 1, No. 3, October 1975 pp 335-348

TABA, H. Curriculum Development Theory and Practice, Harcourt, Brace and World, New York, 1962

THOMAS, L. F. 'Learning and Meaning', in Fransella, F. op.cit, 1978

THOMAS, L. F. and HARRI-AUGSTEIN, E.S. 'Learning to Learn: the Personal Construction and Exchange of Meaning', in Howe, M.J.A. (ed) Adult Learning: Psychological Research and Applications, John Wiley and Sons, London, 1977

THOMAS, L. F., McKNIGHT, C. and SHAW, M. L. G. Grids and Group Structure, Centre for the Study of Human Learning, Brunel University, Middlesex, 1976

TOUGH, A. Learning Without a Teacher, Ontario Institute for Studies in Education, Toronto, 1967

TOUGH, A. 'The Adult's Learning Projects', Research in Education Series No. 1, Ontario Institute for Studies in Education, Toronto, 1971

TOUGH, A. 'Major Learning Efforts: Recent Research and Future Directions', Adult Education Vol 28, No. 4, Summer 1978, pp 250-263

TOYE, M. 'Learning Theory and Education', Paper presented to Third Annual Conference of Standing Committee on University Teaching and Research in the Education of Adults, 12-14th June 1973.

TROWBRIDGE, N. 'Teacher Self Concept and Teaching Style', in Chanan, G. (ed), Towards a Science of Teaching, National Foundation for Educational Research, Slough, Bucks, 1973

WHITEHEAD, A. N. Adventures in Ideas, McMillan & Co., New York, 1929

WITKIN, H. A. et al 'Field-dependent and Field-independent cognitive Styles and their Educational Implications', Review of Educational Research, Vol. 47, No. 1, Winter 1977, pp 1-64.

WRAGG, E. C. Teaching Teaching, David and Charles, Newton Abbot, Devon, 1974

YORKE, D. M. 'Repertory Grids in Educational Research: some methodological considerations', British Educational Research Journal, Vol. 4, No. 2, 1978, pp 63-74.